THE BEAUTY OF

THE BEAUTY
OF HOLINESS

Michael Ashton

O worship the LORD in the beauty of holiness!
Bow down before Him, His glory proclaim;
With gold of obedience, and incense of lowliness,
Kneel and adore Him, the LORD is His name.
John Samuel Bewley Monsell (1811-75)

THE CHRISTADELPHIAN
404 SHAFTMOOR LANE
HALL GREEN
BIRMINGHAM B28 8SZ

First Edition: 2007

ISBN 978-085189172-9

Printed and bound by

THE CROMWELL PRESS
TROWBRIDGE
WILTSHIRE
ENGLAND
BA14 0XB

CONTENTS

PREFACE vii

1. "A Kingdom of Priests ... an Holy Nation" 1

2. Holy and Unholy 7

3. And God Called 13

4. "And the LORD spake" 20

5. Sacrifice and Offering 27

6. "Thou shalt make his soul an offering for sin" . . .35
   Leviticus 4:1–5:13; 6:24-30

7. Forgive us our Trespasses 43
   Leviticus 5:14–6:7; 7:1-10

8. "Present your bodies a living sacrifice" 51
   Leviticus 1:3-17; 6:8-13

9. "Let us offer the sacrifice of praise" 59
   Leviticus 3:1-17; 7:11-34

10. My Meat is to do His Will 67
    Leviticus 2:1-16; 6:14-18

11. "Consider the Apostle and High Priest" 75
    Leviticus 8,9

12. Priests with Infirmity 83
    Leviticus 10

13. Clean and Unclean Meats 90
    Leviticus 11

14. Things from within Defile the Man 98
    Leviticus 12,15

15. Leprosy and Sin 106
    Leviticus 13,14

16. The Day of Atonement .116
    Leviticus 16

17. Separate from the Nations 124
     Leviticus 17,18
18. Crime and Punishment 132
     Leviticus 19,20
19. To whom Much is Given 139
     Leviticus 21,22
20. The Calendar 146
     Leviticus 23
21. Daily Devotion 153
     Leviticus 24
22. Liberty and Jubilee 161
     Leviticus 25
23. Perfecting Holiness 169
     Leviticus 26,27

SUBJECT INDEX 177
SCRIPTURE REFERENCES 180

PREFACE

IN ancient times, a Jewish child began his study of scripture with the book of Leviticus. Today, the book is often neglected, and its message is not understood. Yet important passages from Leviticus are quoted by the Lord Jesus Christ and by his apostles, and incorporated into their teaching. Perhaps therefore our understanding of scripture will be enhanced if we too start by looking at Leviticus, realising that in common with all of the law, it is a schoolmaster to bring us unto Christ and to provide a firm foundation for faith (Galatians 3:24).

The book of Leviticus, with all its priestly commands and ordinances, was given through Moses during the first month of the second year of Israel's Exodus journey. The book turns on two main teachings, which together form "the Royal Law": a) the Holiness of God, and b) what man must do in response in holy living.

The theme of holiness in the Book of Leviticus emphasises the differences between God and man. God is intrinsically holy, while man is of the earth. Yet God wishes to dwell amongst His people so that they will be sanctified. The construction of the tabernacle allowed God to dwell in the heart of the camp, and it was from the tabernacle that He spoke to Moses. He was inviting His people to come to Him, as the Hebrew title of the book indicates: "And He called". In Old Testament times this call was made through God's servants the prophets, who became witnesses of prophecies about the Lord Jesus Christ that were to be fulfilled through his work. God's presence with His people today is through the knowledge of His glory revealed in the Lord Jesus Christ.

1

"A KINGDOM OF PRIESTS …
AN HOLY NATION"

ISRAEL's first year after leaving Egypt was climactic. After Passover night in their blood-protected houses and with their loins girded, the members of the fledgling nation left Egypt, travelling eastwards to the shore of the Red Sea. There, with the waters of the Red Sea before them and Pharaoh's army behind, Moses encouraged them to "Stand still, and see the salvation of the LORD" (Exodus 14:13). What a salvation it was!

"The waters were a wall unto them on their right hand, and on their left … and Israel saw that great work which the LORD did upon the Egyptians."
(verses 29,31)

Just a month later, with their food supplies almost exhausted, God's salvation was all but forgotten:

"The whole congregation of the children of Israel murmured … Would to God we had died by the hand of the LORD in the land of Egypt." (16:2,3)

God sent bread from heaven, feeding them that day and for "forty years, until they came to a land inhabited" (verse 35). Shortly afterwards, they murmured again because there was no water to drink, and God provided water from the smitten rock: a rock that followed them and represented the Lord Jesus Christ (17:6; 1 Corinthians 10:4). He also smote their enemies, the Amalekites, and promised He would be continually at war with Amalek "from generation to generation" (Exodus 17:16).

Only three months out from Egypt, the children of Israel entered the Sinai wilderness, and Moses ascended Mount Sinai to commune with God. The Lord's message was clear (19:4-6):

1. He brought the nation out of Egypt so that His people could be with Him;

1

2. By responding obediently to God's care, Israel would be His special treasure; and

3. They would be "a kingdom of priests, and an holy nation".

God Descended in the Mount

To add to the awesome experiences of those early months in the wilderness, God confirmed His message by descending upon and speaking from the mount to all the assembly:

"There were thunders and lightnings, and a thick cloud upon the mount, and the voice of the trumpet ... the whole mount quaked greatly." (19:16,18)

He set before them principles and laws that confirmed His majesty, and that regulated their social and religious life. By being obedient to these commands, Israel would be drawn ever closer to God.

Yet the events of the three months since leaving Egypt did not bode well for Israel's constancy in matters relating to God. They needed something to remind them regularly of their need for Him, and of the requirements He set before them. Part of God's message therefore instructed them about the organisation of their worship: He gave details of a sanctuary to be made, "that I may dwell among them" (25:8). Surely, they would remain true to His call with this constant reminder at the centre of their encampment of God's abiding presence among them?

The rest of the first year after leaving Egypt was spent preparing all the ornate and decorated parts of this portable sanctuary. In different ways, every member of the nation had an opportunity to be involved. Everyone was encouraged to bring a gift (Exodus 25:2), and under the leadership of Bezaleel and Aholiab various skills and abilities were employed in the tabernacle's construction. There were jobs for workers in metal, wood, leather, cloth and embroidery. The workmanship was to be of the highest quality, as befitted God, who promised to dwell in the heart of the camp.

Explaining the Spiritual Sacrifices

Six months were spent carefully preparing all the different parts of the tabernacle, its vessels, and the garments for the priests; and during all this time the nation remained camped at the foot of Sinai. As they worked, Bezaleel and Aholiab – men filled with wisdom, understanding and knowledge (35:31) – explained the spiritual significance that attached to each part of the work, and how it would be used once the tabernacle was operational, for God put in their heart to teach (verse 34). Yet for six months it was all theoretical; the whole arrangement was still in prospect and not in reality.

Finally, as the anniversary of Israel's leaving Egypt approached, the work was completed:

"... in *the first month* in the second year, on the first day of the month ... the tabernacle was reared up." (40:17)

The theoretical teaching they had received from Bezaleel and Aholiab now had to be put into practice; and with the anniversary of Passover rapidly approaching, there was a lot that needed doing. If the previous twelve months were full of activity, the next month was completely action-packed.

The Presence of God was Central

The book of Leviticus does not contain any dates, and only three specific historical events are mentioned in its pages.* After the book of Exodus, the next date recorded in scripture is in Numbers 1:

"... the first day of *the second month*, in the second year after they were come out of the land of Egypt ..." (1:1)

– when Moses was told to take a census of the people. On the basis of this information, Moses was told to organise the nation by its tribes to form a theocentric camp: one where God would become the focus of attention. Each tribe had an allocated position to pitch its tents. The twelve tribes were arranged in four groups of three; their tents creating a hollow square with a large open area in the centre. This open area was itself surrounded by the tents of the Levites, the central space being reserved for the "tabernacle of the congregation". Wherever any individual

---

* The consecration of Aaron and his sons (chapter 8); the sin of Nadab and Abihu (chapter 10); and the blasphemous man (chapter 24).

was in the camp, the presence of God was central to his life, and the focus of his attention.

From this carefully recorded calendar of events (summarised in the table below), it is apparent that the detailed instructions in the book of Leviticus were all given through Moses during the first month of the second year, while the nation was still camped in Sinai (Leviticus 27:34). He conveyed these to the nation to explain how the tabernacle was to be used, and the underlying purpose of the law. By means of these instructions, the people were taught about God, and how He can be approached.

Worship at the tabernacle was cyclical. Certain tasks had to be performed daily, weekly, monthly, seasonally, and annually. Some events only occurred every third year,

Date	Event	Reference
14th day of 1st month of 1st year	Passover Night	Exodus 12:18
15th day of 2nd month of 1st year	Murmured against God	Exodus 16:1
3rd month of 1st year	Arrived at Sinai Received the law	Exodus 19:1
	Constructed the Tabernacle	
1st day of 1st month of 2nd year	Erected the Tabernacle	Exodus 40:17
During 1st month of 2nd year	**Sacrificial & Priestly commands given in Book of Leviticus**	
1st day of 2nd month of 2nd year	Tribal allocations within the Camp	Numbers 1:1
20th day of 2nd month of 2nd year	Israel leave Sinai	Numbers 10:11

4

every seventh year or every fiftieth year. By giving all this information during the first month, most of the regular tasks were put into practice immediately, reinforcing the message in the minds of those who were involved.

Two Great Teachings

The book of Leviticus is therefore a book with a simple and direct purpose: to teach the nation of Israel about God, and about what the Jews' relationship with Him demanded of them. This purpose is summarised in two passages in the book, and the Lord Jesus Christ in his teaching refers to them both. The main purpose is stated four times in Leviticus, when God says:

> "I am the LORD your God: ye shall therefore sanctify yourselves, and *ye shall be holy; for I am holy.*"
> (Leviticus 11:44; cp. 11:45; 19:2; 20:26)

When Jesus repeated this, he helped to explain what is entailed in being holy, like unto God. He said in the Sermon on the Mount, in the context of not being a respecter of persons:

> "Be ye therefore perfect, even as your Father which is in heaven is perfect." (Matthew 5:48)

Luke's account puts it like this:

> "Be ye therefore merciful, as your Father also is merciful." (Luke 6:36)

The holiness of God, which is such an important theme of Leviticus and of the Bible as a whole is considered in more detail in later chapters. For now we must note that the prime objective of the regulations and ordinances in Leviticus was that Israel would be holy, like unto God, who is "merciful and gracious, longsuffering, and abundant in goodness and truth" (Exodus 34:6). Without the information in the book of Leviticus, the implications of God's holiness would not be so readily understood.

Love Your Neighbour

There was a consequence of this teaching, also picked up by Jesus in the Gospels from a passage in Leviticus. Furthermore, Moses' words emphasise that it is a consequence: there was a requirement placed upon a nation seeking to practise the holiness of God:

"… thou shalt love thy neighbour as thyself: I am the LORD." (Leviticus 19:18; cp. Matthew 19:19, 22:39 etc.)

Love of the Holy God, and love of one's neighbour as a consequence of love for God, become the twin pillars on which the whole of God's law is based, making it "the royal law" as James describes it (James 2:8).

Leviticus was therefore the book for God's royal priests: men and women who sought to worship Him "in the beauty of holiness".

Writing to believers in Christ who were widely scattered through the Roman Empire towards the end of the first century AD, the Apostle Peter stressed the relevance of the theme of God's call to holiness. He expressed this by using language straight out of the books of Exodus and Leviticus:

"Gird up the loins of your mind … as he which hath called you is holy, so be ye holy in all manner of conversation … Ye were not redeemed with corruptible things … but with the precious blood of Christ, as of a lamb without blemish … Ye also, as lively stones, are built up a spiritual house, an holy priesthood, to offer up spiritual sacrifices … Ye are a chosen generation, a royal priesthood, an holy nation, a peculiar people; that ye should shew forth the praises of him who hath called you out of darkness into his marvellous light."

(1 Peter 1:13 – 2:10)

2

HOLY AND UNHOLY

EACH of the sixty-six books of the Bible emphasises a particular aspect of God's revelation to mankind, and our understanding of His purpose would be poorer and incomplete if just one of these books was missing. This is why it is important to read the scriptures frequently and systematically in order to come to know the whole counsel of God. As already demonstrated, the book of Leviticus emphasises God's holiness, and explains how men and women should respond to Him: "ye shall be holy; for I am holy" (Leviticus 11:44).

We also discovered that there are only three historical events recorded in Leviticus. All three are related to the subject of holiness, providing further proof that the book focuses on this subject:

1. The consecration of Aaron and his sons as priests required that they underwent a ritual cleansing in order for them to be considered 'holy'.
2. Aaron's sons, Nadab and Abihu, were killed because they did not maintain the holiness required of them. They ignored God's ordinances and offered strange fire before Him; they failed to distinguish between things that were holy and things that were profane.
3. Finally, there was the case of the man who blasphemed God's holy name, and was stoned at God's command.

Holy Ground and a Holy Day

Holiness is not a subject that is frequently discussed, for it is seemingly unconnected with the affairs of everyday life. Today it is generally understood as referring to a form of unnatural piety: the supposed superiority that comes from claiming to be religious. Outside the Bible, information about holiness is virtually non-existent, yet the subject is vital to a correct understanding of God's message to

7

mankind. As with many Bible words, its first use is instructive, and occurs when Moses drew aside in the desert to see the burning bush. God said to him: "Put off thy shoes from off thy feet, for the place whereon thou standest is holy (Hebrew, *qodesh*) ground" (Exodus 3:5). God spoke to Moses by His angel, and the place of meeting was holy because it was sanctified or hallowed by God's presence.

"Sanctify" and "hallow" translate *qadash*, the verb form of the same Hebrew word; this time it describes something being made or becoming holy. The first use of this verb is even earlier in the Bible account when "God blessed the seventh day, and *sanctified* it" (Genesis 2:3). Here, as with Moses at the burning bush, the underlying idea is of something set apart or made different. The site of the burning bush in the desert was unusual or out of the ordinary; Moses was leaving man's domain and briefly entering into God's. The sabbath day was to be considered as belonging to God; it too was set apart, so that men and women left off their own pursuits to concentrate wholly on the things of God. This is the essence of the meaning of "holiness": something that is separate or set apart.

But there are two further aspects to the subject that are critical to our understanding. First, in both examples – the hallowing of the seventh day, and the burning bush on holy ground – what set them apart was their association with God. Holiness derives wholly and completely from God Himself. He is "the Holy One of Israel" (Psalm 89:18). He swears "by his holiness" (Amos 4:2), just as He swears "by himself" (6:8), indicating that holiness cannot be considered other than in connection with Almighty God. Secondly, though holiness is inextricably associated with God, it always involves an invitation to man. Moses was called to stand before the burning bush; and the holy sabbath, a day to be associated with things divine, was, according to the Lord Jesus, "made for man, and not man for the sabbath" (Mark 2:27).

God's Holy Name

This supports the conclusion already reached by looking at how the word is used in scripture. God is separate from, and above His creation, and particularly from man, yet He reaches out to him. As Isaiah revealed, God's ways and thoughts are far above those of all men and women (Isaiah 55:8,9). What sets God apart from man is His holiness; it is the essence of His character. We often acknowledge that the character of God is revealed in His name with all its moral qualities, and His holiness therefore also has a strong moral aspect. Coupled with the fact that holiness describes God's total 'otherness' from man, this moral dimension shows that God's separation involves His being higher and more elevated in every sense: He is thus "the high and lofty One that inhabiteth eternity". He dwells "in the high and holy place" (Isaiah 57:15), so that as the heavens are higher than the earth, so God in His holiness is higher than man. This elevation is emphasised, not only by referring to heaven as "the high and holy place", but also by an additional term, as if "holiness" by itself is insufficient to explain God's exalted position in relation to man.

The tabernacle and temple in Jewish worship were "patterns of things in the heavens … figures of the true" (Hebrews 9:23,24), and they included a "sanctuary" – a place set apart and made holy – called "the most holy place", or "the holy of holies", where the word for holiness is repeated in the original in order to express the superlative.* Every aspect of the Jewish calendar of worship focused increasing attention on the Holy of Holies, and thus on God Himself. The religious year climaxed on the Day of Atonement, when the high priest was able to enter into the Most Holy Place, which was filled with God's presence and glory. Thus, in the vision Isaiah the prophet saw in the year that king Uzziah died, the seraphim cry out: "Holy, holy, holy, is the LORD of hosts: the whole earth is full of his glory" (Isaiah 6:3). In comparison to this vision of absolute holiness, Isaiah had to declare, "I am a man of unclean lips, and I dwell in the midst of a people of unclean lips" (verse 5).

"Unholy" or "Common"

Leviticus constantly explains this difference between God and man, yet holds out an invitation from God asking men

---

* In the same way as Moses declared to Israel: "The LORD your God is **God of gods**, and **Lord of lords**" (Deuteronomy 10:17).

and women to be holy like Him. He bows down from heaven to earth with the object of lifting up mankind to sit in heavenly places in Christ. Leviticus speaks forthrightly about man and his characteristics. There are descriptions of his bodily functions, his illnesses, his diet, his sexual relations – every part of human life is analysed and considered. Many aspects of daily life can be degrading, and God calls to men and women to lift them out of conditions that can be defiling. Another aspect of the theme of holiness in the book of Leviticus is therefore how it is set in opposition to things that are "common", "profane", or "unholy". As we have already noted, Nadab and Abihu were killed because as priests they should have distinguished "between holy and unholy" (Leviticus 10:10). "Holy" things are those that have to do with God and heaven; "unholy" things relate to the earth, man's domain.*

God's words to Aaron after the death of Nadab and Abihu expand our understanding of the condition described as "common" or "unholy". Aaron was told to "put difference between holy and unholy, *and* between unclean and clean". It is easy to conclude that these two contrasting terms say the same thing; i.e., that "holy" is equivalent to "clean", and "unholy" to "unclean". But the Hebrew word translated "common", "profane" or "unholy" (*chol*), simply refers to conditions, things or people that are not holy. Although this word, like "holiness", has its verb (*chalal*), meaning to profane, pollute, defile or desecrate, "common" things are not necessarily polluted or defiled, but they are susceptible to defilement because they exist in a polluted and unholy environment.

The following table shows how the words "holy" and "unholy" are related to each other as contrasting states, and how the "unholy" or "common" state can be subdivided

---

* Supporting the suggestion the God's holiness and His appeal to man to be holy like Him is the central theme of Leviticus, the word "Holy" and its associated terms occur 152 times in the book, and "profane" occurs 14 times (in both cases providing 20% of all uses in the Old Testament); "unclean" and its associated terms occur 132 times in the book (over 50% of the Old Testament total); "clean" and its related words appear 74 times (35% of the total).

God	Man	
Holy	Unholy	
	Clean	Unclean

into "clean" and "unclean". The fact that the "Holy" state is not susceptible to a similar subdivision emphasises the inviolability of Almighty God, "with whom is no variableness, neither shadow of turning" (James 1:17), and contrasts Him to man who is constantly faced by the choice between good and evil. God's appeal to holiness stands in stark contrast to the earthly temptations that lead so easily to evil thoughts, words and actions.

Because holiness is so fundamentally associated with God, and unholiness with man, the call to holiness is even more amazing. Its achievement also seems destined to failure. The message of Leviticus, which points forward unmistakably to the work of the Lord Jesus Christ, is therefore highly encouraging, for true holiness is only possible through him. In the New Testament, Jesus is described before his birth as "that holy thing", when the angel Gabriel explained to Mary about the child she would conceive by the power of the Holy Spirit (Luke 1:35). And after his death and resurrection, Peter told the crowds who gathered in Jerusalem for Pentecost that they had "denied *the Holy One* and the Just ... and killed the Prince of life" (Acts 3:14,15). The resurrection was the great proof of Jesus' victory, for he was "declared to be the Son of God with power, according to the spirit of holiness, by the resurrection from the dead" (Romans 1:4).

The pursuit of holiness is so important, that the Apostle told the Hebrews to "follow peace with all men, and holiness, without which no man shall see the Lord" (Hebrews 12:14). The message of Leviticus contains God's message about how to follow holiness.

It will be helpful at this juncture to summarise Bible teaching about holy and unholy:
- The primary meaning of "holiness" is 'separation', 'different', 'otherness'.

- Only God is intrinsically holy; holiness therefore derives from Him; He is its source.
- Because God is holy, holiness essentially involves moral qualities.
- The call to holiness is an invitation from God to lift mankind above and out of the conditions of the sinful world.
- Man's world is naturally "unholy" or "common".
- The human condition can be further subdivided into "clean" and "unclean".

Important words in Leviticus	Hebrew
Holiness (noun)	*qodesh*
To sanctify (verb)	*qadash*
Sacred, holy, saint (adjective)	*qadowsh*
Unholy, common, profane (noun)	*chol*
To profane, pollute, defile, desecrate (verb)	*chalal*
Clean (noun)	*tahowr*
To clean, purify, purge (verb)	*taher*
Unclean, defiled, polluted (adjective)	*tame*
To defile, pollute, become unclean (verb)	*tame*

3

AND GOD CALLED

THE Holy God revealed Himself to Moses in the burning bush, and invited him to be His messenger to His captive people. It looked as if He might continue to speak in that way, for after the children of Israel were redeemed from Egypt God spoke to them from mount Sinai, "the mount ... that burned with fire" (Hebrews 12:18). Yet the experience was so frightening, they asked not to hear from God directly in the future, saying to Moses: "Speak thou with us, and we will hear: but let not God speak with us, lest we die" (Exodus 20:19). During the first months of the wilderness journey, Moses fulfilled this request by taking his own tent and pitching it "without the camp". There, outside the camp, "the LORD talked with Moses" (Exodus 33:7-11).

This information is recorded immediately after the chapter that recounts Israel's sin in the matter of the golden calf, and this explains why Moses had to go outside the camp to meet with God. The people had "sinned a great sin", and God promised to "visit their sin upon them" (32:31,34). Sin is defiling and degrading; and if God were to walk in the midst of the camp, the camp and its inhabitants needed to be holy (see Deuteronomy 23:14).

Was God abandoning His People?

As Moses was in the process of moving his tent outside the camp, the people were obviously apprehensive about what might happen. Because of their sin, they must have wondered if God was going to abandon the people He had redeemed from Egypt. Those fears were quickly removed, because "as Moses entered into the tabernacle, the cloudy pillar descended, and stood at the door of the tabernacle, and the LORD talked with Moses" (Exodus 33:9). The pillar of cloud was the reassurance the people needed. Moses

13

mediated acceptably on their behalf, and God was gracious to His people and put away their sin.

Yet, although it was necessary because of sin for Moses to pitch his tent outside the camp, this was far from ideal. God did not wish to be distant or separated from His people; He wanted to be in their midst, in the heart of their camp. He therefore gave Moses instructions about another tabernacle* that the people were to prepare: "Make me a sanctuary (Hebrew, *miqdash*, a holy or sanctified place) that I may dwell among them" (Exodus 25:8). This holy place would only be temporary, for God had already revealed that He was leading Israel to a land prepared for them; and Moses was able confidently to say: "thou shalt bring them in, and plant them in the mountain of thine inheritance, in the place, O LORD, which thou hast made for thee to dwell in, in the Sanctuary, O LORD, which thy hands have established" (Exodus 15:17).

But until the nation entered the Holy Land, God promised to be with and among them as they travelled. Exodus 40 recounts the occasion when the tabernacle was first erected in the centre of the camp – not outside its boundaries – and how "a cloud covered the tent of the congregation, and the glory of the LORD filled the tabernacle" (Exodus 40:34). Only then, and from a sanctuary constructed faithfully "according to the pattern shewed to (Moses) in the mount" (Hebrews 8:5; Exodus 25:40), did God speak through Moses to the people from the midst of the camp. The dramatic opening words of Leviticus describe this historic occasion: "And the LORD called unto Moses, and spake unto him out of the tabernacle of the congregation" (Leviticus 1:1).

"Moses was not able to enter"

When Moses pitched his tent outside the camp, he entered the tent and the pillar of cloud representing God's presence "stood at the door". This situation was reversed when the tabernacle constructed to God's pattern was made. That tabernacle was filled with the glory of God by

---

* Moses' tent outside the camp is always described using the Hebrew word *ohel*, a tent. The tabernacle that became a sanctuary is often called a *mishkan*, a dwelling, expressing how it would be used by God.

the covering cloudy pillar of fire, "and Moses was not able to enter into the tent of the congregation, because the cloud abode thereon, and the glory of the LORD filled the tabernacle" (Exodus 40:35).

The fact that Moses was not allowed to enter the tabernacle might give the impression that God wished to distance Himself from His servant Moses and from the children of Israel. But, in fact, the opposite is true. The whole arrangement was designed as a gracious invitation to the people of God. That is why the tabernacle was erected in the centre of the camp. But God's holiness could not be compromised; He was available to every member of the nation, but they had to approach Him with reverence and awe. To stress this constant invitation from God to His people, the Book of Leviticus in the Jewish Bible has the title, "And He Called" (Hebrew, *wayyiqra*), taken from the opening word in the original text of Leviticus 1:1. This reinforces the information already gleaned from a consideration of the holiness of God, that a major aspect of holiness is the implicit invitation that God extends to mankind. God's call was to everyone, and the information that follows in the book of Leviticus explained how men and women were to approach God acceptably, with joy and not with fear.

Relating to the Levites

The Jewish title is therefore particularly appropriate, and much more relevant than "Leviticus" as found in English Bibles. The English name comes originally from the Septuagint (Greek) translation of the Old Testament, which gave the book the name *Leueitikon*, meaning 'relating to the Levites'. The title was then adopted by the Latin Vulgate version as *Liber Leviticus* (the book relating to the Levites), and finally the English translators used it. This title is somewhat misleading, as we have seen, for the message is aimed at *all* the people of God, not just the tribe of Levi. Even if it is argued that the regulations and commands are especially relevant to those who were being charged to uphold them, then the book is more for the priests the sons of Aaron than for all the tribe of Levi, even though the Apostle describes the priesthood as "Levitical" (Hebrews 7:11).

15

Another reason why the Jewish title is helpful is that it emphasises the close connection of Leviticus with the other books of Moses. The opening word (*wayyiqra*) starts with what Hebrew scholars call a '*waw* conjunctive'. This breaks all the rules of modern grammar where a sentence – to say nothing of a chapter or a book – ought not to start with the word 'And'. But no book of the Bible ever stands completely alone. Leviticus carries on immediately where Exodus leaves off, and therefore it is right that the first verse should start, "*And* the LORD called ..." Furthermore, Leviticus is linked unmistakably to Numbers, the book that follows it in the canon of scripture, for Numbers too starts with a '*waw* conjunctive': "And the LORD spake ..." (Numbers 1:1). In both Leviticus and Numbers, God spoke out of the tabernacle in the wilderness. He spoke to His people through Moses, who "verily was faithful in all his house, as a servant, for a testimony of those things which were to be spoken after" (Hebrews 3:5).

To become Facts at a later Stage

Here, in the Apostle's words, lies the importance of the book of Leviticus for the modern disciple. What was said and done during the wilderness journey was "a testimony of ... things ... to be spoken after", or, as Brother Fred Barling helpfully paraphrased it, "bearing prophetic witness to matters which would become facts at a later stage".* A study of Leviticus will show us what was required of God's people in the Mosaic dispensation as they travelled through the wilderness and when they entered the land God had prepared for their habitation; but much more importantly these requirements were prophecies to be fulfilled through the Lord Jesus Christ. The people of God in the Christian dispensation are not different from their Jewish counterparts in Moses' day; they face the same issues, and have the same needs. These needs find their fulfilment in those matters which became facts in the life and work of our Lord. Now that Jesus has come, there is no excuse – no one ought to read Leviticus without seeing his shadow cast across every chapter and every verse.

---

* From *Hebrews – A Thematic Study of the Epistle*, 1954, published by the author.

16

This great truth is brought to the fore right at the beginning of the Letter to the Hebrews, the book that is the New Testament companion of – and commentary upon – the Book of Leviticus. A comparison of the opening verses of the two books shows clearly how the coming of Jesus Christ was foreshadowed in Israel's experiences in the wilderness. God, who before had spoken through His prophets, and in Moses' day "out of the tabernacle", now speaks through His Son:

"And the LORD called unto Moses, and spake unto him out of the tabernacle of the congregation, saying, Speak unto the children of Israel." (Leviticus 1:1,2)

"God, who at sundry times and in divers manners spake in time past unto the fathers by the prophets, hath in these last days spoken unto us by his Son." (Hebrews 1:1,2)

The Link with Hebrews

This link between Leviticus and Hebrews teaches us that the One who speaks in Leviticus is the same God who in "these last days" has spoken to us through His Son. Although there are important contrasts between living under the provisions of the law and living in the grace of the Lord Jesus Christ, important connections between the shadows in the Law and the substance that is Christ must not be destroyed. Therefore, although the Old Testament book carries an English title meaning that it relates to the Levites, we ought not to conclude that it has no relevance at all for believers in Christ. Many of the wonderful teachings in Hebrews depend on a reader's familiarity with the Mosaic law, and in particular with the law as revealed in Leviticus.

God did not speak to Moses from out of the tabernacle using words that could be ignored or treated capriciously. He *"called* unto Moses", and it was a summons or appeal to the people to draw near to Him. Yet for many who read Leviticus today, even many who have embraced the Gospel of Christ, the wording of His call in Leviticus is not attractive; they are not drawn closer to God by the material in the book, but feel distant from Him and perplexed by many of His commands recorded in the law. The objective of this book, therefore, is to show the relevance of the message of Leviticus for today's disciples of Christ, and to draw the unmistakable links between God's message to the nation of Israel in the wilderness, and His message to followers of the Lord Jesus who are in a wilderness of probation endeavouring to enter fully into God's promised rest.

The Continuing Presence of God

One aspect of Leviticus is particularly helpful in showing the strong message that is for believers in every age. Throughout Leviticus, God is present with His people. He is not a God far off, but one who is near and who is interested in their welfare. We sing in one of our hymns, "O God, unseen yet ever near" (Hymn 239). But for Israel, God's presence was not only visible in "the shadowing cloud by day, the moving fire by night" (Hymn 112), it was also tangible. The offerings on the altar were partially *His* bread, i.e., His food (Leviticus 21:6, etc.). As the priests took the offerings brought by the people, they approached "before the LORD" (16:1) as before an all-powerful Monarch. Those who sought to approach on their own terms forfeited their lives.

But even more than in their religious observances and in their offerings, God was present and concerned with every aspect of their daily lives. He constantly reminded them, "I am the LORD your God" (19:3), whenever they were being instructed about acceptable behaviour in their relationships with one another. Their behaviour to others should reflect His behaviour towards them. He was their redeemer, and they ought to become redeemers for their brethren. For fear and reverence of Him, consideration should be shown to all in need. God reminded the nation that He is aware of men's needs, and He expects His people to relieve those needs if at all possible.

This continuing presence of God is emphasised by each commandment and instruction in Leviticus. Yet while it is true that God was permanently present with His people, just as He is "not far from every one of us: for in him we live, and move, and have our being" (Acts 17:27,28), Leviticus also teaches about special national occasions when God was visibly present in glory. These occasions were related to the fact that a sign of His presence in the tabernacle showed His covenant relationship with Israel. He told Moses: "There I will meet with the children of Israel, and the tabernacle shall be sanctified by my glory" (Exodus 29:43).

The Apostle John was therefore able to say of the Lord Jesus Christ, "the Word was made flesh, and dwelt among us (and we beheld his glory, the glory as of the only begotten of the Father), full of grace and truth" (John 1:14). God is permanently present with His people today, and cares for them just as He did for Israel in the wilderness. But His glory is no longer revealed to us dramatically or visibly in a fiery cloud or in the abiding glory that shone from between the cherubim. The evidence is much more personal: "God … hath shined in our hearts, to give the light of the knowledge of the glory of God in the face of Jesus Christ" (2 Corinthians 4:6).

4

"AND THE LORD SPAKE ..."

W E have seen that the great theme of the book of Leviticus is holiness: the holiness of God, and Israel's call to be holy like unto Him. This call issued from the dwelling place God commanded to be constructed in the midst of Israel's encampment, and was delivered to Moses during an intense period of activity in the first month of the second year after Israel left Egypt. The message was for each individual Israelite, but was delivered through Moses, their divinely appointed leader. The book opens with God calling to Moses from out of the tabernacle (Leviticus 1:1), and continues with a record of God's conversations with His servant, noted by the recurring phrase, "And the LORD spake unto Moses, saying ...", with which each new section of the book commences.*

God's message to Moses was primarily intended for the nation as a whole, but its implementation was often placed in the hands of Aaron and his sons, who were appointed by God to represent the nation before Him. One particular section of the book (chapters 11–15, sometimes called 'The Law of Purification') is specifically addressed to Moses *and* Aaron: "And the LORD spake unto Moses *and to Aaron*, saying ..." (11:1; 13:1; 14:33; 15:1). This emphasises a critical role for the priests, for God made it "a statute for ever throughout your generations ... that ye may put difference between holy and unholy, and between unclean and clean; and *that ye may teach* the children of Israel ..." (10:9-11). The priests were obviously intended to instruct the people in matters of holiness.

---

* This phrase occurs 33 times in Leviticus: 4:1; 5:14; 6:1,8,19,24; 7:22,28; 8:1; 11:1; 12:1; 13:1; 14:1,33; 15:1; 16:1; 17:1; 18:1; 19:1; 20:1; 21:16; 22:1,17,26; 23:1,9,23,26,33; 24:1,13; 25:1; 27:1.

God's Message to Moses

In chapter 17, God asks Moses to speak directly to "Aaron, and unto his sons, and unto all the children of Israel" about the importance of offering correctly on the altar of sacrifice (17:2). Once again, the priests bore responsibility to ensure that everything was done decently and in order. It is also apparent from these examples that the opening phrase of each section in Leviticus contains important details that explain the purpose of the message. These phrases act as sub-headings throughout the book.

The dialogue style – God speaking to Moses, and Moses speaking to the people and the priests – is only abandoned on the three occasions when specific historical events are reported as if by a narrator:

1. The consecration of Aaron and his sons is introduced by the phrase, "and Moses brought ..." (8:6-36).
2. The sin of Nadab and Abihu: "And Nadab and Abihu, the sons of Aaron, took each (RV) of them his censer, and put fire therein ..." (10:1-7).
3. The blasphemous man: "And the son of an Israelitish woman, whose father was an Egyptian ... blasphemed the name of the LORD" (24:10-12).

The Central Position of the Day of Atonement

One of God's conversations with Moses was directly related to the first of these events. Leviticus 16 opens with the following words: "And the LORD spake unto Moses *after the death of the two sons of Aaron*, when they offered before the LORD, and died" (16:1). As the death of Nadab and Abihu is recorded in chapter 10, it is apparent that the account in chapter 16 is deliberately relegated to a later stage, and follows the account of 'The Law of Purification'. Chapter 16 describes the Day of Atonement: the one day each year when the High Priest, as the representative of the whole nation, was able to enter into the Most Holy Place. It was the pinnacle and aim of Israel's relationship with their God. He dwelt among them, and through their High Priest they responded to His gracious invitation to dwell with Him.

Approach to God could only be on the basis of conditions that He determined; therefore before the details of the

THE BEAUTY OF HOLINESS

Day of Atonement were recorded, Israel received instructions about the laws of sacrifice and purification, and the establishment of the priesthood. But equally, there were important consequences that flowed from this close relationship between God and His people; so the section that follows focuses on 'The Law of Holiness', and its application to the various aspects of daily life within Israel. God was inviting His people to share fellowship with Him, therefore the details surrounding the Day of Atonement separate the book of Leviticus into two main sections: first, the conditions needed for fellowship to exist; and secondly, the obligations of fellowship. By noting where different introductory phrases occur, and acknowledging the central role of the Day of Atonement, the basic structure of Leviticus quickly falls into place (see table below).

ANALYSIS OF LEVITICUS

A. The Conditions for Fellowship
(chapters 1-15)
- The Law of Sacrifice (chapters 1-7)
    - For the People (chapters 1-5)
    - For the Priests (chapters 6,7)
- The Inauguration of the Priesthood (chapters 8-10)
  [The Sin of Nadab and Abihu, chapter 10]
- The Law of Purification (chapters 11-15)
- The Day of Atonement (chapter 16)
- The Law of Offerings (chapter 17)

B. The Obligations of Fellowship
(chapters 18-27)
- The Law of Holiness (chapters 18-27)
    - For the People (chapters 18-20)
    - For the Priests (chapters 21,22)
    - The Religious Calendar (chapters 23-25)
      [The Blasphemous Man, chapter 24]
    - Blessing & Cursing (chapter 26)
    - Voluntary Gifts and Vows (chapter 27)

For Priests and People

With this simple structure in mind, there are further details that help to expand our understanding of the book's objective. Clearly, the information it contains was vital for Aaron and his sons. They were appointed as priests, and were to play a crucial role in teaching the nation about God and His ways: "For the priest's lips should keep knowledge, and they should seek the law at his mouth: for he is the messenger of the LORD of hosts" (Malachi 2:7). The information contained in Leviticus was certainly vital for the priests, but it had an infinitely wider application: it was also vital for all the people. The priests could not keep it to themselves, for many of the commands were directed specifically to everyone else in Israel.

This twofold purpose is apparent as soon as the detail of the book is considered. The section on 'The Law of Sacrifice', for example, is in two parts. In the first place, Moses was told to "Speak unto *the children of Israel*, and say unto them, If any man of you bring an offering unto the LORD ..." (Leviticus 1:2). Chapters 1-5 expand on this by explaining the different offerings that a man could bring. But in chapter 6:8,9, Moses turns from speaking to the people to speak to his brother Aaron: "*Command Aaron* and his sons, saying, this is the law of the burnt offering ..." Here and in the next chapter, Moses sets out the priestly requirements and involvement in the various sacrifices that the people were to offer to God.

Equally, in 'The Law of Holiness' there is a section addressed specifically to the people (chapters 18-20): "*Speak unto the children of Israel*, and say unto them, I am the LORD your God (18:2); followed by one directed to "*the priests* the sons of Aaron" (chapters 21,22).

The Failure of the Priests

This reveals that the book is God's invitation to every individual in Israel. Each man and woman was being told of his or her need for mediation and sacrifice in order to approach God acceptably. For their part, Aaron and his sons were told of the vital role they were to play in bringing men and women closer to their God. Chapters 8–10 explain the appointment of the priests, and include details of how they were made both representative of, and separate from everyone else in Israel. Yet, immediately after the inauguration of the priests is the account of Nadab and Abihu's transgression. It was a warning to all subsequent generations of Aaronic priests that the position they held by natural descent demanded from them the highest standards of personal commitment and obedience. The laws of purification, the details of which follow immediately the account of Nadab and Abihu's rebellion, therefore applied as much to them as to the common people. Aaron and his remaining sons were instructed never to "drink wine nor strong drink ... when ye go into the tabernacle of the congregation ... that ye may put difference between holy and unholy" (10:9,10). The first laws of purification thus explain the differences between clean and unclean animals, so that each Israelite – including the priests – could appreciate on a daily basis that discrimination and separation are required of all the people of God (11:1-47).

The failure of Nadab and Abihu was also prophetic. They were part of the first generation to be anointed priests after Aaron, and the Aaronic priesthood was based on "the law of a carnal commandment" (Hebrews 7:16), that is, human descent. The intrinsic weakness and certain failure of the Levitical priesthood was therefore evident right from the beginning, and the thoughtful Israelite would doubtless ask what he was to do if fellowship with God was dependent on sacrifice and mediation, when it was so apparent that the mediators were fatally flawed!

The Failure of the People

The problem was even more serious. For, lest it be thought that the potential for failure rested only with the priests, the second part of Leviticus containing 'The Law of Holiness' also records an account of failure. On this occasion it is one of the common people who does not follow God's commands: "the son of an Israelitish woman, whose father was an Egyptian ... blasphemed the name of the LORD" (Leviticus 24:10,11). This showed how each individual would have to acknowledge that, if the priesthood was susceptible to failure, it must also be true of the nation as a whole, for as a later prophet would write, "it shall be, like people, like priest" (Hosea 4:9, RV).

The actual ordinances of the law thus pointed to their inadequacy to achieve their stated objective, and to the desperate need for a better priest, better sacrifices, and a better covenant. This is how the law led men and women to see the need for the Lord Jesus Christ. The underlying objective of the law could not be faulted: it was "holy, and just, and good" (Romans 7:12), but it was "weak through the flesh" (8:3) and doomed to failure. As we consider the message of Leviticus, we must therefore always seek to understand the role of the law, for it was fulfilled in Christ, even though his disciples have been freed from the constraints of its detailed commands.

The Religious Year

There are two further divisions in the 'Law of Holiness' section that we have not thus far considered. After the provisions for the people (chapters 18-20) and the provisions for the priests (chapters 21,22), there is a description of the annual religious calendar (chapters 23-25). This was inaugurated when the children of Israel came out from Egypt, and Passover marked "the beginning of months: it shall be the first month of the year to you" (Exodus 12:2). Passover and the Feast of Unleavened Bread were kept by Israel during their wilderness wanderings, but other parts of the calendar would apply fully only after they entered into the Land and were living an agricultural life. Chapter 25 provides details of the Year of Release (the Sabbath year) and the Jubilee, occasions of great rejoicing when the people could remember all that God had done for them.

The concluding chapters (26,27) explain how God would bless the nation for following His commands and statutes, and they warn of the dire consequences that would flow if Israel turned away from God's ways. Though Leviticus contains many of God's commands, His intention was that the children of Israel would wish to serve Him willingly – that they would acknowledge the great difference between bondage in Egypt and living under the beneficent care of the God of all the earth. Many commentators have puzzled over the final chapter in Leviticus, and have failed

25

adequately to describe its purpose or its place in the overall structure of the book. Yet it surely emphasises the "Holiness" theme of Leviticus, as witnessed by the recurring phrases in the chapter: "shall be holy"; "shall sanctify"; "Holy unto the LORD", etc. God wants men and women to be holy like unto Him, but He cannot command, demand or dictate holiness. God seeks *willing* servants, *faithful* subjects, *selfless* children. The structure of national life revealed by the laws and ordinances in Leviticus was intended to impress on each man and woman in Israel the need for personal and individual devotion to God. He asked them to follow Him and obey His word because they wanted to and delighted to, not grudgingly because He commanded it.

5

SACRIFICE AND OFFERING

THE first section of Leviticus contains detailed descriptions of offerings that were to be sacrificed to God by the children of Israel. For various reasons it is difficult for modern disciples to understand or appreciate the importance and significance of animal sacrifices. Everything about such sacrifices is alien to our present way of life; very few who live in the Western world are personally involved in the killing of animals for food, and many find the practice of animal sacrifices repulsive. Whereas those who received these commands lived closer to the land, and were less squeamish than today's city dwellers, they too must have questioned the purpose and meaning of the sacrifices, particularly as so many different details were given in connection with a variety of offerings.

First of all, as we have previously commented, information about the sacrifices was given in two parts: one directed to the people who brought the offerings (Leviticus 1:1–6:7), the other to the priests who officiated at the tabernacle (6:8–7:38). Both these sets of directions deal with the various different offerings, of which there were six, made up of three pairs: sin offering and trespass offering, burnt offering and peace offering, meal offering and drink offering.

Information for People and Priests
The first thing to be noticed is that the separate information for people and priests does not follow an identical pattern. In the people's list, the peace offering has a central position, whereas it comes last in the list given to the priests. The people were shown that all the offerings had a central objective: peace or fellowship with God; and the priests were shown that this blessed

27

People		Priests	
Burnt offering (*olah*)	1:3-17	Burnt offering	6:8-13
Cereal (meal) offering (*minchah*)	2:1-16	Cereal (meal) offering	6:14-18
Sacrifice (*zebach*) of peace offering (*shelem*)	3:1-17	Sin offering	6:24-30
Sin offering (*chatta'ah*)	4:1–5:19	Trespass offering	7:1-10
Trespass offering (*'asham*)	5:14–6:7	Peace offering	7:11-34

situation is the outcome of a process, and is dependent on certain prerequisites.

Secondly, though we have mentioned six offerings, only five are specifically mentioned in Leviticus 1–7. The 'missing' offering is the drink offering, and no details about this are given until Numbers 15:1-16. The information given in Numbers, however, shows that a drink offering always accompanied the cereal offering, and it must therefore be considered as an intrinsic part of that offering. Another factor that arises from the details about the cereal and drink offerings is that they were never offered on their own. Not only were they always offered together, they always accompanied other offerings, as necessary adjuncts. The offerings they accompanied were the burnt offering and the peace offering. The children of Israel could not offer cereal and drink offerings with either their sin offerings or their trespass offerings.

The Order of the Offerings

There is one other detail to bear in mind before drawing some conclusions about the general teaching of the law of offerings, and this concerns the order in which sacrifices were to be offered. If more than one sacrifice was involved, no deviation was permitted from the following order:

28

1. Sin offering
2. Trespass offering
3. Burnt offering ⎤
                  ⎬— Cereal and drink offering
4. Peace offering ⎦

The reason for this rigid order is apparent once we acknowledge man's needs when he approaches before God. Man's greatest problem is sin; and God's greatest gift is the gift of salvation through the sacrifice of His Son. Our sins need covering if we are to approach our loving Heavenly Father, and an offering has been provided to make atonement for our sins, hence the sin offering is first in the list.

Forgiveness of sins, wonderful though it is, is only the first step in a process of binding man back to God. "He is faithful and just to forgive us our sins" (1 John 1:9) only when we confess them and seek to bring our lives into closer conformity with the pattern set by His Son. This is acknowledged in the trespass offering, which had always to be accompanied by some restoration or repayment, commensurate with the damage (i.e., the trespass) that had been done.

Even confessing his sin and trying to mend his future ways were only early steps on the Israelite's road back to God. His Father looked for him to dedicate and commit *all* his future life to God's will, and this was marked by bringing a burnt offering that was to be *wholly* consumed on the altar. Then, and only then, could a sacrifice be made for a peace offering. This showed that man cannot share fellowship with God when he remains deep in sin, and has taken no steps to remedy the damage his sin has caused, or has failed to commit himself wholly to God's ways.

Works of Righteousness and Joy
We have seen that the cereal and drink offerings were only associated with the burnt offering and the peace offering. Why could they not be offered with either the sin offering or the trespass offering? Meat (food) and drink speak of man and his works, as Jesus said: "My meat is to do the will of him that sent me, and to finish his work" (John

29

4:34). In the law of the offerings the Israelites were not encouraged to celebrate their selfish sinful deeds, but to engage in works of righteousness and joy in association with their commitment to God and their fellowship with Him.

There is thus a logical and divinely appointed order of offerings revealed in the law, and it can be set out as follows:

1. Sin offering for atonement
2. Trespass offering for modification
3. Burnt offering for dedication
4. Peace offering for fellowship
5. Cereal and drink offerings expressing righteousness and joyfulness

This list effectively reduces the six offerings to five, but there is another detail to be considered that further reduces the number. Leviticus 7:7 explains, "As the sin offering is, so is the trespass offering: there is one law for them". This does not mean, as we have seen, that the purpose of the two offerings was identical, but that the "law" and the instructions about presenting them were identical. It was therefore possible to comprehend the whole law of the offerings by referring to a schedule comprising four sacrifices: sin offerings (i.e., sin and trespass), burnt offering, peace offering, and the cereal offering (with its associated drink offering).

Four Major Offerings

This summary of four offerings becomes important for today's disciples because of a comment made in the Psalms that is also quoted in the Letter to the Hebrews:

> "Sacrifice and offering thou didst not desire; mine ears hast thou opened: burnt offering and sin offering hast thou not required." (Psalm 40:6)

What is not immediately apparent in our English translation is that this passage contains the Hebrew words for each of the four major offerings. "Sacrifice" translates the Hebrew word *zebach*, meaning peace offering; and "offering" translates *minchah*, the word for a cereal offering. So the verse actually reads: "Peace offering and cereal offering thou didst not desire ... burnt offering (*olah*) and sin offering (*chata'ah*) hast thou not required."

While noting the reference in Psalm 40 to the four main divisions of the law of offerings, we must not overlook what this important verse is saying about offerings in general. Despite all the information given through Moses to Israel, and all the details that applied to the children of Israel and their appointed priests, the Psalmist says that God did not require these offerings from them. Nor is this an isolated verse in the scriptures. Samuel explained to Saul that "to obey is better than sacrifice, and to hearken than the fat of rams" (1 Samuel 15:22); and Hosea revealed that God "desired mercy, and not sacrifice; and the knowledge of God more than burnt offerings" (Hosea 6:6). Offerings are thus to be regarded as an indication of something much more important, that affects believers in the modern age and in the Christian dispensation just as much as it did the nation of Israel living under the Law of Moses in Old Testament times.

For the psalmist goes on to say:

> "Lo, I come: in the volume of the book it is written of me, I delight to do thy will, O my God: yea, thy law is within my heart." (Psalm 40:7,8)

He uses here an unusual word for "heart", which is translated elsewhere as "bowels" (e.g., Psalm 22:14) and describes man's internal organs. These "inward parts" represent man's central purpose: the aim and direction of his life. According to the law of the offerings, these parts in sacrificed animals received special treatment, and were reserved for God Himself:

> "The fat that covereth the inwards, and all the fat that is upon the inwards, and the two kidneys, and the fat that is upon them, which is by the flanks, and the caul above the liver, with the kidneys ... the priest shall burn them upon the altar: it is the food of the offering made by fire for a sweet savour: all the fat is the LORD's." (Leviticus 3:14-16)

"Truth in the inward parts"

It was fitting that these parts should be sacrificed to God and not shared with either the person who brought the

31

THE BEAUTY OF HOLINESS

offering or with the officiating priest, for David speaks in another Psalm about the importance of man's inward parts in this way:

> "Behold, thou desirest truth in the inward parts: and in the hidden part thou shalt make me to know wisdom." (Psalm 51:6)

By devoting our energies and the aim of our lives to the things revealed in God's word, we give ourselves – sacrifice, or offer ourselves – to Him, and become the "living sacrifices" which the Apostle described to brethren and sisters in Rome (Romans 12:1).

The message of the offerings is therefore as valid today as it was for Israel of old. The sacrifice God requires is the willing commitment of men and women, who follow Him from their hearts, and whose innermost being yearns for Him.

This teaching about wholehearted commitment that is an intrinsic part of the law of the offerings highlights an enormous problem for *all* men and women, not only those who lived under the law's demands. No one is able fully to live up to its requirements. Bringing to God the animals He required was an admission of a man's needs, but without the perfection God demanded, the position of the one making the offering was unchanged. In the Letter to the Hebrews, the Apostle acknowledges this dilemma, but he approaches it from a different direction. He writes about the deficiency in the animals rather than about the failings of those who brought them to be offered. "It is not possible", he says, "that the blood of bulls and of goats should take away sins" (Hebrews 10:4). A yawning gap remained between what the sacrifice was meant to symbolise and the actual life of the man or woman who brought it to the priest; also there was no logical connection between the death of an animal and the benefit sought by the person who sacrificed it.

On the same grounds, the prophet Micah asked the question:

> "Wherewith shall I come before the LORD, and bow myself before the high God? Shall I come before him with burnt offerings, with calves of a year old? Will the

LORD be pleased with thousands of rams, or with ten thousands of rivers of oil?" (Micah 6:6,7)

The animals were merely representative; they stood in the place of the person who brought them to be sacrificed. As a man laid his hand on the head of an animal to identify himself with his offering, it would be apparent to him that he was not being fairly represented. If the sacrifice was a sin offering, how could a spotless bullock stand in lieu of one who was admitting his imperfections in the very act of presenting the sacrifice? It would not matter if he brought one animal or many; as the scriptures indicate, the blood of thousands of rams could never take away sins.

Unable to take away Sins

For modern disciples who are not expected to sacrifice animals, the bullocks, rams and lambs can be replaced with a list of other sacrifices, such as showing kindness, sharing hospitality, and doing good to all. Such acts can fill a man's life and involve great personal sacrifice, but they can never take away sins. It is possible to give up worldly ambition, to devote one's life to the care of a loved one, or renounce fame and fortune. But the most generous and selfless philanthropist is as much a sinner after he has given all, as he was before ever he first tried to help his neighbour.

It is in this context that Psalm 40 is quoted in Hebrews 10. The Apostle noted the Psalmist's words, explaining how God took no pleasure in the animal sacrifices of the law, viewing them in isolation. He acknowledged that God looked for willing and obedient service more than He did for perfect and spotless offerings; He wanted a people who would remain devoted to His ways. But the history of His covenant people was no different from the history of all other nations, and the divine commentary was unremitting: "They are all gone aside, they are all together become filthy: there is none that doeth good, no, not one" (Psalm 14:3). Whereas this was true of all God's creation, yet the Psalmist was able to speak of one to come, who would say: "Lo, I come to do thy will, O God" (40:7, cited Hebrews 10:7,9).

33

Because the Lord Jesus Christ was "the Lamb of God (slain from the foundation of the world), which taketh away the sin of the world" (John 1:29; Revelation 13:8), the Apostle was able to conclude his commentary on Psalm 40 by saying that through Jesus' obedience, "we are sanctified through the offering of the body of Jesus Christ once for all" (Hebrews 10:10). Here was a sacrifice God required; here was *the* sacrifice God required. The Lord Jesus' willingness to fulfil what was written of him "in the volume of the book" made him a spotless offering – the only one able to take away sins. His was a perfection that was different from the outward spotlessness demanded of animal sacrifices; he was morally spotless – in the inward parts. The Psalmist summed up the Lord's attitude: "I delight to do thy will, O my God: yea, thy law is *within my heart*" (Psalm 40:8). His one offering was effective, where the many animal sacrifices under the law were not able to take away sins.

The Lesson of the Offerings

While Jesus' sacrifice meant that the shadowy animal sacrifices of the law were no longer required, the means of approach to God still involves the steps that the children of Israel were taught as they tried to follow the details set down in Leviticus. Disciples of Christ do not need to offer a sacrifice for sin in order to receive forgiveness, but they acknowledge the efficacy of Jesus' sacrifice each time they confess their sins. God does not ask them to make an offering whenever they commit a trespass, but He does expect them wherever possible to make generous reparation, and by amending their ways to try not to fail in the same way in future. He encourages them to be more wholly committed to Him, and offers through Christ the benefits of fellowship, divine comfort and protection, and the promise of eternal righteousness and rejoicing in the kingdom age. These are the lasting lessons of the law of the offerings, and they are as relevant today as when they were first given.

6

"THOU SHALT MAKE HIS SOUL AN OFFERING FOR SIN"

Leviticus 4:1–5:13; 6:24-30

WHEN we considered the sacrifices required by the Law of Moses, we discovered that the children of Israel were instructed to bring animal offerings to God in order to learn of their personal needs as God's children, and about how these needs could only be met satisfactorily by Him. They were powerless to resolve their own problems, and needed to rely wholly on His mercy. In return, what He demanded from them was "mercy, and not sacrifice" (Hosea 6:6). The sacrifices thus had a dual purpose, as did the law itself. They showed unmistakably that something better than a system of animal offerings was required to take away sins, but they also indicated the method God would use and the principles upon which He would act to redeem mankind from sin and death.

The Lesson of the Offerings

Regarding the offerings themselves, the New Testament scriptures explain how "it is not possible that the blood of bulls and of goats should take away sins" (Hebrews 10:4); it needed "the precious blood of Christ, as of a lamb without blemish and without spot" (1 Peter 1:19). We can also see how each offering, in general terms, contains an important teaching that still applies today:

1. As sinners, we rely on the sacrifice God provided in order to make atonement and reconciliation, and we acknowledge through faith and baptism that this sacrifice was fulfilled in the laying down of the life of His Son, our Lord Jesus Christ (the sin offering).

2. In praying to God to "forgive us our trespasses, as we forgive those who trespass against us", we also acknowledge the need each person has to learn from past mistakes, and to try wherever possible to repair any damage caused by those mistakes (the trespass offering).

35

3. This demands that we try to live our lives more completely in service to God, responding to His gracious invitation by humbly submitting to His will in every circumstance and at all times (the burnt offering).

4. The Father's response is to welcome us into covenant relationship, with all the benefits that fellowship can bring (the peace offering).

This general teaching drawn from the offerings leads us also to look at the details of the various sacrifices. Although believers in Christ are not required to bring the offerings that formed part of the Israelites' service, the details have been preserved because they teach equally important principles that can help us to live more acceptably before God. These details, as well as the overall message of the offerings, reinforce the two lessons already detected:

• the need for a better sacrifice, and
• the principles underlying God's acceptance of sinful mankind.

The Need for Balance

These two messages of the law of sacrifice are so closely linked that it is wrong to emphasise one at the expense of the other; the scriptures always keep both aspects in perfect balance. It is possible, for example, to point out all the limitations of the law and draw the conclusion that it contained nothing of value whatsoever. A slightly less extreme view sees the law as fulfilling its purpose for Israel as a nation, but with no abiding message for believers in Christ other than its complete unsuitability.

There is also another extreme. This acknowledges the fact that the law was a schoolmaster to bring men and women to Christ, and weighs each detail carefully to show how completely the Lord Jesus Christ was prefigured in the law. The logical development of this view is that the information in the New Testament is largely superfluous. According to this view, the Aaronic priests were exact shadows of Christ and his mediatorial work, and the only difference from the Melchizedek priesthood was the mortality of Aaron and his sons.

This is not the way New Testament writers, including the Lord himself, speak about the law. They make clear the fact that the law was of limited value: "as a vesture shalt thou fold them up, and they shall be changed" (Hebrews 1:12). But the underlying lessons of the law remain vitally true; and they are taught in matters both great and small – in the overall picture and in the detail.

These two aspects are revealed when we look at the sin offering, the first offering in the whole cycle. This sacrifice was required of "the children of Israel" (Leviticus 4:2) both individually and collectively, whenever it became apparent that they had "done somewhat – through ignorance (verse 2) – against any of the commandments of the LORD concerning things which should not be done, and are guilty" (verse 13). But what about other sins? What of sins committed knowingly and repeatedly? What of "adultery, fornication, uncleanness, lasciviousness, idolatry, witchcraft, hatred, variance, emulations, wrath, strife, seditions, heresies, envyings, murders, drunkenness, revellings, and such like" (Galatians 5:19-21)? However diligently we comb through the law of the offerings there is no sacrifice for offences like these; there was simply no provision under the law for the habitual or deliberate sinner. Indeed, it is certain that every man and woman in Israel committed in their lifetime at least one sin which the sin offering was powerless to cover, such was the law's serious limitation.

Dependence upon God's Mercy

David knew this when he lost himself with Bathsheba, and said: "Thou desirest not sacrifice; else would I give it" (Psalm 51:16). He knew that there had to be something better, and besought God:

> "Have mercy upon me … according to thy lovingkindness: according to the multitude of thy tender mercies blot out my transgressions. Wash me throughly from mine iniquity, and cleanse me from my sin." (verses 1,2)

Jesus confirmed that David's request was not fanciful, his merciful Father could also forgive these other sins: "I say unto you, *All manner* of sin and blasphemy shall be forgiven unto men" (Matthew 12:31).

Though David understood that there was no sacrifice under the Law of Moses for his sins, and that if God were to forgive him it would be on a different and better basis, he also knew that the Mosaic sacrifices were instructive:

"Behold, thou desirest truth in the inward parts ... the sacrifices of God (i.e., the ones He does desire) are a broken spirit: a broken and a contrite heart, O God, thou wilt not despise." (Psalm 51:6,17)

The details of the sin offering are therefore important for us, even though we rely on the better sacrifice of Christ.

The first thing to be noticed is that different offerings were required from different classes of people. No one in Israel, high-born or low-born, was exempt from these requirements (see table below).

The various animals did not differentiate between different sins, for "all unrighteousness is sin" (1 John 5:17); they simply marked the different status of the person who was making the offering and ignored the exact nature of his sin. The offerings reduced in value depending on the position in the nation of the one making the offering: the priests and the nation itself offered the most costly animal, a bullock, and the poorest of the people only had to bring a handful of flour. Two principles

Priest	Bullock	4:3
Whole Nation	Bullock	4:13,14
Ruler	Kid Goat (male)	4:22,23
Commoner	Kid Goat (female)	4:27,28
Poor	2 Pigeons or Turtledoves	5:7
Very Poor	A tenth of an Ephah of Flour	5:11

were involved, and they still have force today. The first is the principle of responsibility: "unto whomsoever much is given, of him shall be much required" (Luke 12:48). The priests were the channels by which the word of God came to the people. They should have known the law and its responsibilities; and if they disobeyed its commands they were particularly culpable. The second principle was that, due to their position, priests and rulers could lead by showing either a good or bad example, and the consequences of their actions could be very far-reaching indeed. This was indicated in the law of the sin offering, which said: "if the anointed priest shall sin so as to bring guilt on the people ..." (Leviticus 4:3, RV).

We should also notice that sin offerings, like the other sacrifices under the law, were for God's covenant people: for Israel, and its priests and rulers. Men and women of other nations could only benefit if they renounced all former associations and adopted the Jews' religion. This is what made John the Baptist's declaration about Jesus so remarkable: "Behold the Lamb of God, which taketh away the sin *of the world*" (John 1:29).

Important Differences

Not only were different animals required from the different classes of people who offered them, the various animals were also handled differently. This can be seen in the contrast between a priest sacrificing a bullock and a ruler sacrificing a goat. Of all the sin offerings, only the blood of bullocks was sprinkled "before the LORD, before the vail of the sanctuary" (Leviticus 4:6,17). Some of its blood was also put on the horns of the altar of incense in the holy place, and the rest was poured out at the base of the altar of burnt offering in the tabernacle court (verses 7,18). When a goat was sacrificed, however, its blood did not enter the tabernacle at all: it was smeared on the horns of the altar of burnt offering, and poured out at its base (verse 25).

The carcases of the two animals also received different treatment. With the priests' or nation's bullock, its inward fat was burnt on the altar, and everything else was carried outside the camp to be completely consumed by fire (verses 8-12). The treatment of the ruler's goat appears at first to be the same. Its inward fat was burnt on the altar (verse 25), but the flesh was not taken outside the camp as the bullocks' flesh was taken; the priests ate it: "in the holy place shall it be eaten, in the court of the tabernacle of the congregation", i.e., beside the altar of burnt offering (6:26). This act of eating the flesh of sacrifices offered to God was the acme of fellowship, as the Apostle Paul revealed to the Corinthians: "Do ye not know that they which minister about holy things live (i.e., feed, margin) of the things of the temple? And they which wait at the altar are partakers with the altar? (1 Corinthians 9:13).

These differences are not easily spotted as we read about the sacrifices in Leviticus, but they are clearly important, for the Apostle refers to them in his letter to the Hebrew believers. He explains:

"We (i.e., believers in Christ) have an altar, whereof they have no right to eat which serve the tabernacle. For the bodies of those beasts, whose blood is brought into the holy place by the high priest as an offering for sin, are burned without the camp."

(Hebrews 13:10,11, RV)

As members of the priesthood, Aaron and his sons did not share in Christ's sacrifice. Their fellowship was with a system that identified sins, but did not take them away. Would they ever have wondered why the flesh of the bullock that was offered on behalf of the sins of the nation was burned outside the camp, and no portion was available for them to eat? Israel was being taught in a graphic fashion that the law could only bring men and women as far as the altar. It revealed sin as the great adversary of mankind, and showed how sins must be forgiven if men and women are to draw close to God.

Reliance on the law was shortsighted, and ignored the fact that it was impotent to save. It had to be discarded and left behind. The Apostle therefore challenged the Hebrews: "Let us go forth therefore unto him without the camp, bearing his reproach" (Hebrews 13:13).

The Shedding of Blood

But what would the faithful and thoughtful Israelite make of the law of the sin offering? In times of national disobedience he would see a bullock being slain and the

40

blood drained from the carcase. The main action with the blood was to take it inside the tabernacle and right up to the entrance to the most holy place. He was informed that here, immediately before the sanctuary, the high priest splashed the blood on the veil and smeared it on the horns of the altar of incense. When the animal was cut open, the inward part was burned on God's altar, and the rest of the carcase was taken outside the camp to be completely destroyed by fire.

Only with the sin offering was the blood 'splashed' (Hebrew, *nazar*, meaning to spurt or spatter); the blood of the other offerings was 'sprinkled' or 'scattered' (Hebrew *zaraq*, Leviticus 1:5). This dramatic action reinforced the great truth first revealed in the Garden of Eden, when the Lord God slew an animal to "make coats of skins, and clothed them" (Genesis 3:21), leading the Apostle to declare: "without shedding (Greek, *ekcheo*, meaning 'pour out', 'shed forth') of blood is no remission" of sins (Hebrews 9:22).

With the burning of the fat, Israel was being shown that God was seeking the inward man: his heart, his emotions and intellect, and his devotion. When these are directed to spiritual ends in a person's life, they are a "sweetsmelling savour" to God. By contrast, when God instructed that the bullock's carcase be destroyed, He showed Israel, as Jesus later declared, that "it is the spirit that quickeneth; the flesh profiteth nothing" (John 6:63). The Apostle Paul declared: "that no flesh should glory before God" (1 Corinthians 1:29, RV). He also commented specifically on the destruction of the carcase of the sin offering when he wrote to the Romans about baptism into Christ:

> "Our old man is crucified with him, that the body of sin might be destroyed, that henceforth we should not serve sin." (Romans 6:6)

This clearly links sin with mortality, and mortality with sinfulness, as Paul points out in the previous chapter:

> "By one man sin entered into the world, and death by sin; and so death passed upon all men, for that all have sinned ..." (5:12)

Primarily, of course, the sin offering was not foreshadowing what was required of believers, but what the Lord Jesus Christ would achieve in his life and by his death. It was *his* blood that was to be shed, as the prophet Isaiah predicted: "he hath poured out his soul unto death" (Isaiah 53:12). It was Jesus who acknowledged that "the flesh profiteth nothing", when he willingly allowed himself to be taken and nailed to the tree, "without the camp". He knew that God looks on the heart, and that his Father had already declared, "This is my beloved Son, in whom I am well pleased" (Matthew 3:17). For these reasons, the prophet was able to say about God not requiring an animal sacrifice from David:

"It pleased the LORD to bruise him; he hath put him to grief: when thou shalt make his soul an offering for sin … the pleasure of the LORD shall prosper in his hand."   (Isaiah 53:10)

MAIN POINTS OF THE SIN OFFERING

- animals of different value were sacrificed depending on the offerer's position within the nation: a kid for individuals or a bullock for the whole nation
- special provision was made for the poor, who could bring birds, or even flour
- sin offerings for the whole nation were treated differently from those for individuals: the blood was taken into the tabernacle, the fat was burned on the altar, and the carcase was completely burned outside the camp
- this looked forward to the offering of Jesus, who died outside the city, yet his life was accepted by God because Jesus devoted himself completely to God's will
- the flesh of offerings made by individuals was eaten by the priests within the tabernacle court
- by receiving the fat burned on the altar, God showed that He wants man's inner devotion
- the destruction of the carcase outside the camp showed that "the flesh profiteth nothing"

7

FORGIVE US OUR TRESPASSES
Leviticus 5:14–6:7; 7:1-10

"If ye forgive men their trespasses, your heavenly Father will also forgive you: but if ye forgive not men their trespasses, neither will your Father forgive your trespasses."   *(Matthew 6:14,15)*

TRESPASS is not a word in regular use today. It seems archaic, and is equated in many people's minds with notices on private property saying: "Trespassers will be Prosecuted", or with the Lord's Prayer as they once learned it at school: "… forgive us our trespasses, as we forgive those that trespass against us". In this latter connection the word is understood to be an alternative way of saying 'sin'. However, there are important differences between sins and trespasses. The Apostle John tells us that: "sin is the transgression of the law" (1 John 3:4); and Paul that to sin is to "come short of the glory of God" (Romans 3:23). Both the Old Testament and New Testament words for sin, *chatta'ah* and *hamartia*, carry this sense of 'missing the mark' and falling short.

Sin and Trespass

A "trespass" is different. Certainly, to commit a trespass is to commit a sin; but while all trespasses are sin, not all sins are trespasses. When a trespass is committed, there is always another party involved, or some damage occurs. This is apparent when the trespass offering is introduced in Leviticus:

> "If a soul sin, and commit a trespass against the LORD, and lie unto his neighbour in that which was delivered him to keep, or in fellowship, or in a thing taken away by violence, or hath deceived his neighbour; or have found that which was lost, and lieth concerning it, and sweareth falsely …"   (Leviticus 6:2,3)

43

A few examples of acts that are described in the scriptures as trespasses illustrate that a trespass involves damage to a third party:

- Adultery invades the rights of a husband or wife (Numbers 5:12,27)
- The Philistines who captured the ark invaded God's privacy (1 Samuel 6:4)
- Idolatry robs God of the service due to Him (2 Chronicles 24:18)

These examples show that it is possible to commit trespasses against both God and man, and this is confirmed in Leviticus where details are given about the trespass offering. Leviticus 5:14-19 describes the offering that was required in cases of trespass against God, and 6:1-7 the offering that was to be brought when a trespass had been committed against man.

In considering the sin offering, we learned that different animals had to be offered depending on a person's standing in the nation (see page 38).

This list did not include the option of a male sheep – a ram, which is surprising. But as soon as the trespass offering is considered, the reason is immediately apparent: the two offerings cannot be considered completely separately. As the directions for the priests confirm, "as the sin offering is, so is the trespass offering: there is one law for them" (7:7). Under the law there was only one animal appropriate for a trespass offering: "a ram without blemish" (5:15,18; 6:6). This indicated that, so far as guilt is concerned, there is no difference between one person and another, so rich or poor, high born or low born had to offer a ram. Only one animal in the schedule of beasts that were acceptable for offerings was of greater value than a ram: and that was a bullock. Many in Israel would find it hard to afford a ram. God made concessions for the very poor who brought sin offerings to Him, but He required a ram in every case of trespass.

To make matters worse, in addition to the ram being free from blemish, it also had to be of an acceptable value, in proportion to the seriousness of the trespass: "according to thy estimation in silver by shekels, after the shekel of the sanctuary" (5:15, RV). By Jewish custom, the plural "shekels" meant that the ram had to be worth at least two shekels – i.e., be at least two years old – and if a more valuable animal was required, this was to be determined by the priests "after the shekel of the sanctuary", in order to avoid any attempt at deception by the use of false weights and measures.

The emphasis on a single acceptable offering shows that God does not distinguish between one trespass and another. There was an acknowledgement that different degrees of damage may result, but the essential guilt is no different: another person has been violated.

The animal was taken by the priest, to "make an atonement for him" (5:16), showing that the trespass was forgiven, and the blood was sprinkled "round about upon the altar" (7:2). Apart from how the blood was handled, the priests dealt with the trespass offering as they did with the sin offering: the fat and all the inwards were wholly burnt on the altar, and the flesh was eaten by the priests in "a holy place" (7:6, RV, cp. 6:26). As we have learned (page 39), the blood of the sin offering was splashed, not sprinkled, and in one particular case it was taken right to the veil in front of the Most Holy Place. The blood of trespass offerings never entered the tabernacle; it was simply sprinkled round the altar.

Repaying More than the Damage

Even a ram was not sufficient by itself to clear the slate completely for a man who had committed a trespass. By bringing an offering, he received atonement once he acknowledged his crime , but God still expected more from him. An equally important part of the trespass offering was the repayment of any loss or damage resulting from his actions. Where this damage was not immediately obvious, the loss was to be estimated by the person making the offering, and to this he was to "add the fifth part" (5:16). It was not enough in God's sight to make full restitution; the trespasser must go beyond this in admitting that his action was wrong. There is no explanation in the text of why the additional amount should be a fifth part, though some commentators have pointed out that it is comparable to a double tithe, and

45

therefore indicates that the act was both wrong in itself, and did wrong to someone else.

However, there is another provision under the law, which also involves adding the fifth part, and this introduces an interesting possibility about its inclusion in the trespass offering. God asked His people to sacrifice the firstborn of all animals to Him as a way of remembering how He brought His firstborn people out of Egypt (Exodus 13:11-16). But this only applied to "clean" animals. God took no pleasure in the sacrifice of unclean beasts, so the firstborn of these animals were to be redeemed, or bought back. The unclean animal was valued "according to thy estimation" (Leviticus 27:27; cp. the same phrase in 5:15 relating to the trespass offering), and a fifth part was added. The thoughtful Israelite would surely realise that, because he had been redeemed by God from Egyptian bondage, the unclean animal actually represented him! God bought him back, and graciously paid more than he was worth, as He does for us through the gift of the Lord Jesus Christ: "for by grace are ye saved through faith; and that not of yourselves: it is the gift of God" (Ephesians 2:8).

It Pays to be Honest

When a man who committed a trespass admitted his fault, he was to be equally gracious towards the person on whom he inflicted damage or loss. God encouraged him in the way of holiness to "add the fifth part", and thus acknowledge the need to mend his ways, and not act like that in future. Other parts of the law were much more onerous, and there is an important lesson to be learned by making the comparison with other situations where repayment was demanded. If a man's possessions were stolen, for example, the thief was required under the law to "restore five oxen for an ox, and four sheep for a sheep" (Exodus 22:1). The difference between the law of the trespass offering, and this case of theft is that the thief tried to hide his crime. When he was caught, the punishment he received was judicial. The trespass offering was different; it was made when a person became aware of his guilt, not when another person discovered his sin. The law therefore emphasised that it pays to be honest; it would be much more costly for the person who tried to conceal his crime.

This vitally important element of repayment in the trespass offering, as well as the sense of the original Hebrew word, has led some translators to provide alternative renderings. Here are some of them:

- "guilt offering" (RSV, NIV, NEB, NASB)
- "reparation offering" (REB)
- "sacrifice of reparation" (JB)
- "penalty" (Tanakh)
- "compensation" (ESV)

As the trespass offering had to be made by each Israelite when he became aware that he had violated a third party, the element of compensation was clearly intended to focus his mind on the damage he had inflicted. He was caused to do all in his power to repay. Furthermore, this did not only apply to physical damage; it was possible to commit a trespass against God just as much as against man.

Trespasses against God

This is illustrated in the case of lepers. Diagnosis of the disease led immediately to the leper being declared ritually unclean: "he shall dwell alone; without the camp shall his habitation be" (Leviticus 13:46). Isolation and quarantine limited the potential of the disease spreading to others, and periodic examination by the priest revealed when the danger of infection had passed. Only then could the leper re-enter the camp. On his return, he was to bring (among other things) a he-lamb – a ram – "for a trespass offering" (14:12).

What trespass had the leper committed? Who had he wronged? The answer lies in his being out of the camp of Israel during the period of his illness. For that length of time he was not one of the "kingdom of priests" or a member of the "holy nation" (Exodus 19:6). As a result of his disease, God was robbed of his service while he was excluded from the fellowship of other Israelites and from national worship. The trespass offering was to acknowledge this period of lost service, and he should also seek to make reparation.

The same was true of a Nazarite who failed to fulfil the complete period of time that he promised to devote himself to God's service. He acknowledged the wrong done to God by bringing a trespass offering (Numbers 6:12).

These and other examples show how the law brought home forcefully human failure, making men and women in Israel aware of their sinfulness in God's sight. Therefore, the Apostle Paul commented in Romans:

> "The law is holy, and the commandment holy, and just, and good. Was then that which is good made death unto me? God forbid. But sin, that it might appear sin, working death in me by that which is good; that sin by the commandment might become exceeding sinful."
>
> (7:12,13)

You may well be thinking, as all these details are rehearsed, what is the relevance for today's disciples? The Law of Moses no longer applies, and God no longer expects animal sacrifices from His people. While this is true, we noted earlier that the provisions in the law always teach two important lessons: the imperfection of all the offerings under the law, pointing to the need for a better and more effective sacrifice; and the emphasis upon the principles whereby God is prepared to accept sinful men and women.

These lessons also arise when we consider the trespass offering. When we confess our sins, God "is faithful and just to forgive us our sins, and to cleanse us from all unrighteousness" (1 John 1:9); but He still expects us to amend our lives, and to be generous in restitution when we have wronged another person. God's grace in forgiveness places a responsibility upon us, not only to be forgiving ourselves, but also to demonstrate practically the basis on which His forgiveness has been extended to us. Also, just like those in ancient Israel, we can be guilty of withholding from God those things that are due to Him: our praise, honour and worship. Though we are not asked to bring offerings, we ought to be keenly aware of our responsibilities, and grieved at heart when we are less than faithful servants.

"A trespass offering for sin"

We are not asked to offer a ram, because there was no way that a ram, however free it was from blemish, or however valuable "after the shekel of the sanctuary", could atone for the guilt of a man or woman in Israel who had committed a trespass. God provided something of immeasurably greater value when He gave His Son to atone for our sins. The prophet Isaiah revealed that Jesus was given as a trespass offering. He wrote: "It pleased the LORD to bruise him; he hath put him to grief: when thou shalt make his soul an offering for sin" (Isaiah 53:10). "An offering for sin" is literally, "a trespass offering (Hebrew, *'asham*) for sin". To understand exactly what the scriptures are teaching, it is necessary to compare closely the prophet's words and the law of the trespass offering. In Leviticus 6:2, we read: "If a soul sin, and commit a trespass against the LORD ... in a thing taken away by *violence*, or hath *deceived* his neighbour ...". Note carefully those two words "violence" and "deceit". The trespass occurred when a third party was violated; something was done deceitfully, or violence was used.

Isaiah says prophetically of the Lord Jesus:

"He made his grave with the wicked, and with the rich in his death; although (RV) he had done no *violence*, neither was any *deceit* in his mouth. Yet it pleased the LORD to bruise him ... when thou shalt make his soul an offering (a trespass offering) for sin." (Isaiah 53:9,10)

There could be no better offering. Jesus could not be charged with violence or deceit; for Isaiah had earlier said of him: "He shall not cry, nor lift up, nor cause his voice to be heard in the street ... he shall bring forth judgment unto truth" (42:2,3). The great paradox, however, was that in the process of being the trespass offering provided by God for our sins, Jesus' enemies used both deceit and violence against him. He was tried on trumped up charges supported by false witnesses; and he was cruelly scourged and crucified.

A Lesson about Forgiveness

This introduces us to the side of the subject of trespass that was not covered in the law. All that the law did was to encourage the man or woman who committed a trespass to acknowledge his or her guilt and to make generous reparation. God's offering of Jesus was from the One against whom trespasses have been committed. The loving and merciful example of our Heavenly Father and of His Son should encourage today's disciples to act graciously towards those who trespass against them. In this context, Jesus told his parable about the two debtors, where the unforgiving servant was delivered to the tormentors. The Lord concluded the story with this powerful lesson:

"So likewise shall my heavenly Father do also unto you, if ye from your hearts forgive not every one his brother their trespasses." (Matthew 18:35)

MAIN POINTS OF THE TRESPASS OFFERING

- trespass offerings recognised that sins often cause damage to a third party
- only one animal could be used, whatever form the trespass took – an unblemished ram
- as well as bringing the ram, full repayment of any damage was required, plus the addition of "a fifth part" as further compensation
- if a man did not admit his trespass, he was treated as a criminal and had to repay the damage four or five-fold
- trespass offerings taught the need to take responsibility for sinful actions, and to amend behaviour by drawing closer to God

---

8

"PRESENT YOUR BODIES
A LIVING SACRIFICE"
Leviticus 1:3-17; 6:8-13

IN the previous two chapters, we have considered the
sin offering and the trespass offering; every Israelite
had to offer these, for "all have sinned, and come short
of the glory of God" (Romans 3:23). But the burnt offering,
which we shall look at now, and the peace offering which
we consider in the next chapter, were both voluntary
offerings for each individual in Israel. God encouraged all
the people to realize the significance of the burnt offering;
He hoped they would choose to devote themselves to Him,
and show this devotion in their offerings. But they had to
be given willingly:

"He shall offer it of his own voluntary will at the door
of the tabernacle of the congregation before the LORD."
(Leviticus 1:3)

Further to encourage faithful Israelites, burnt offerings
were sacrificed continually on behalf of the entire nation.
As daily sacrifices they were the foundation of the
religious calendar, and were offered in addition to any
others that were required on special or feast days. This is
why the burnt offering is the first one mentioned in the
book of Leviticus, whose opening verses summarise a
longer section in Exodus 29:38-42, where Aaron and his
sons are given instructions about their priestly tasks.

As the burnt offering was to be voluntary, a degree of
latitude was allowed in the choice of animal: it could be a
beast from the herd or from the flock, or a fowl, reflecting
to a large degree the range of offerings allowed in cases of
sin (see table overleaf). The implication is that a person's
standing in the nation should help him determine the
value of the burnt offering to be brought before the Lord.

Sin offering		Burnt Offering	
Priest/Nation	*Bullock*	*Male Bullock*	1:3
Ruler	*Male goat*	*Male goat / lamb*	1:10
Commoner	*Female goat / lamb*	—	
Poor	*2 Doves / pigeons*	*Doves / Pigeons*	1:14
Very poor	*Handful of flour*	—	

A Sweet Savour

Each of these offerings was to be –

"a burnt sacrifice, an offering made by fire, of a sweet savour unto the LORD."   (1:9,13,17)

"Burnt sacrifice" translates the Hebrew word *olah*, meaning literally "to ascend".* The sacrifice – in the form of its "sweet savour" – was to rise up before God. By putting his hand upon the head of the animal before it was sacrificed, the person who offered it associated himself directly with the animal, and he thus expressed his own desire to draw near to God and give Him pleasure (1:4). There is an early example of this when Noah and his family were saved from destruction and brought to a new beginning. Noah –

"builded an altar ... and offered burnt offerings on the altar. And the LORD smelled a sweet savour."

(Genesis 8:20,21)

It was literally, as the words suggest, "an offering sent upwards", but only the pleasing odour – something completely insubstantial – arose before God; everything else was totally consumed.

In making his offering, Noah was indicating deep gratitude for the salvation achieved on his behalf. Before partaking of God's good gifts, he sacrificed a burnt

---

* *Olah* is consistently translated "burnt sacrifice" or offering in the Old Testament, apart from two occasions where an alternative is given. In 1 Kings 10:5 the Queen of Sheba marvels at "the ascent" by which Solomon went up to the temple; and Ezekiel 40:26 describes the seven steps "to go up" to the future temple. In both cases, the details of physical worship express how dedication involves being elevated through association with the things of God.

offering, as though to say: 'Everything comes from God's hand and belongs to Him; this is merely a token, offered in deep thankfulness, and to show the honour due to His great Name'. God's smelling the sweet savour therefore becomes a scriptural metaphor expressing the idea that the Father favourably receives the offering, and by extension He also receives the person who makes the offering in faith and obedience.

The other aspect of the burnt offering, as already mentioned, was the fact that it was *completely consumed*. Alongside the description of it being an offering "of a sweet savour", it is also called "an offering made by fire unto the LORD" (Exodus 29:41 etc.). In fact, anything burnt on the altar was both "of sweet savour" and consumed "by fire". In the case of the burnt offering, however, it was *totally* consumed. What was placed on the altar was offered directly to God, and it became acceptable to Him by becoming a "sweet savour". The burning sacrifice did not represent the consuming of something that was unacceptable in God's sight, but rather the opposite. The totally consumed sacrifice represented what God is pleased to accept: the obedient and willing commitment of His creatures who choose to worship Him in spirit and in truth.

Inspecting and Cleansing

Because the burnt offering indicated a person's wish to dedicate himself to God, great emphasis is placed on the preparation and inspection of the sacrificial animal. The beast was first flayed – its skin was removed and handed to the officiating priest for his own use (Leviticus 7:8), and not returned to the person who brought the offering. The sacrifice was to be given completely, and even though God is not concerned with outward appearances (cp. 1 Samuel 16:7), no physical benefit was to accrue to the person bringing the offering. Once the animal had been skinned, its carcase was separated into parts that were carefully examined and washed. The whole animal had to be completely free from any blemish. While the animal was being washed, particular attention was paid to the inwards and the legs. The lesson must have been plain to the person who brought the animal to be sacrificed. By placing his hands on the animal's head, he had identified himself with the animal; and when he saw careful attention being paid to the inwards and legs, he must have realized that God is concerned with the inner man, and with the direction of his life. All the careful washing would show him that before anyone can dedicate himself to God, he must try to cleanse his ways.

David acknowledged this when he wrote a psalm to commemorate the forgiveness he received in the matter of Bathsheba. Knowing that God had forgiven his sins, and blotted out his iniquities, he said:

"Create in me a clean heart, O God; and renew a right spirit *within me.*" (Psalm 51:10)

The Hebrew word *qereb*, which he uses here, appears in Leviticus 1:9 and elsewhere as "inwards". David asked God to cleanse his innermost being so that he could dedicate himself more completely to God's service, and so that his ways could be more closely aligned to God's ways. Later in Psalm 51, David describes burnt offerings as "sacrifices of righteousness" (verse 19), which is why they could only be offered after a person had acknowledged his sin by bringing a sin offering, and after he had started to amend his ways by bringing a trespass offering. Righteousness involves putting ourselves right with God, and this can only be done acceptably through association with the Lord Jesus Christ, who – like a careful priest – "searcheth the reins and hearts" (Revelation 2:23).

"Sharper than any two-edged sword"

This emphasis on washing and inspection comes out again when the principles of the law are discussed in the letter to the Hebrews. Disciples of Christ are to subject themselves to the searching inspection of God's word, which is –

"quick, and powerful, and sharper than any two-edged sword, piercing even to the dividing asunder of soul and spirit, and of the joints and marrow, and is a discerner of the thoughts and intents of the heart." (Hebrews 4:12)

The word of God is deeply cleansing, allowing us in faith to approach near unto God:

"Let us draw near with a true heart in full assurance of faith, having our hearts sprinkled from an evil conscience, and our bodies washed with pure water."

(10:22)

As we discovered previously when looking at the sin and trespass offerings, God no longer requires animal sacrifices; Jesus brought the Law of Moses to its natural conclusion by becoming himself both sacrifice and priest. But the principles of the offerings still apply, and they are clearly identified in other parts of the scriptures. The Apostle Paul in his letter to the Romans, for example, explains the lesson of the burnt offering that is still relevant and necessary today:

"I beseech you therefore, brethren ... present your bodies a living sacrifice, holy, acceptable unto God, which is your reasonable service."   (Romans 12:1)

Like the Israelites of old, we have a choice set before us. We can choose to accept the forgiveness of sins that God offers us through the work of the Lord Jesus Christ; and we can, if we wish, go no further. But God expected something else from the Israelites. He expected them to learn from the trespass offering about the need to amend their ways; He offered to help them conquer temptation and live as men and women who rejoiced in the new life into which they had entered.

But there was something more still, symbolised by the voluntary burnt offering. God encouraged His people to dedicate themselves to His service, wholly and completely. He knew that it would involve effort and cost, but this is a feature of dedication, where a person's willingness is marked by the expenditure of time and energy. David summed it up when he insisted on buying the threshing floor from Ornan the Jebusite as a site for the altar of burnt offering for Israel:

"I will verily buy it for the full price: for I will not take that which is thine for the LORD, nor offer burnt offerings without cost."   (1 Chronicles 21:24)

"Laid out in order"

The animal chosen as a burnt offering had to be provided by the person making the sacrifice, whether it was an expensive bullock or the more affordable sheep or goat, but whichever animal was killed, the process of sacrificing it was the same. The skin was removed and discarded, and the carcase was divided into parts for examination and cleansing. Then the parts were laid out on the altar. This was not done haphazardly, for we are told repeatedly that the priests laid them "*in order* on the wood that is on the fire which is upon the altar" (Leviticus 1:8,12). The order to be meticulously followed was first of all the head, then the internal fat that surrounds the kidneys and liver, and finally the rest of the body including the legs.

What was God teaching His people by asking them to sacrifice their burnt offerings in this fashion? Clearly He was seeking above all an *intelligent* response; He demanded that the head be laid first on the altar. This was recognized in the Apostle's words to the Romans that we have already considered:

"Present your bodies a living sacrifice ... which is your *reasonable* service."   (Romans 12:1)

The Greek word here is *logikos*, implying that God seeks from us "an act of intelligent worship", as J B Phillips paraphrases the verse. This does not discount our emotional involvement, of course, but emphasizes the fact that the Gospel message has to be understood before it can be acceptably adopted.

The head was followed on the altar by the internal fat, symbolising man's inner being. Devotion to God may start with learning about Him and the way of truth, but this truth has to enter deep into his heart if the whole man is to be converted. Last on the altar was placed the rest of the body, including the animal's legs, acknowledging that our bodies are always the servants of our minds and affections. Paul therefore exhorted the Colossians:

"Set your affection on things above, not on things on the earth."   (Colossians 3:2)

This was necessary in order to be pleasing to God and to show how they were truly "risen with Christ".

This order of head (mind or intelligence), internal fat (affections and desires), and body occurs in another Old Testament passage that is carried over into the New

Testament. Moses summed up the purpose of the law when he said:

"Thou shalt love the LORD thy God with all thine heart, with all thy soul, and with all thy might."
(Deuteronomy 6:5)

The association of this summary with the details of the burnt offering was appreciated by the scribe whose encounter with the Lord is recorded in Mark 12. After Jesus had told him that Moses' summary was "the first of all the commandments", the scribe acknowledged that the Lord had accurately identified the law's focus:

"Master, thou hast said the truth: for there is one God; and there is none other but he: and to love him with all the heart, and with all the understanding, and with all the soul, and with all the strength, and to love his neighbour as himself, is more than all whole burnt offerings and sacrifices." (Mark 12:32,33)

The Continual Burnt Offering

As noted earlier in this chapter, there was a daily burnt offering for the nation as well as burnt offerings for individuals who chose to dedicate themselves to God. The daily offering was offered morning and evening: one lamb at the beginning of the day, and another at the day's end. This sacrifice was called "the *continual* burnt offering" (Exodus 29:42; Numbers 28:3), and all other burnt offerings were patterned on it. It was "continual" because the carcase of each animal slowly consumed over a 12-hour period before being replaced:

"It is the burnt offering because of the burning upon the altar all night unto the morning." (Leviticus 6:9)

Whenever an Israelite brought his own animal to be sacrificed, the continual burnt offering would be slowly burning away; one lamb was *always* there.

There can be no doubt what this represented to Israel of old, and what it teaches us today. Abraham explained to Isaac that, "God will provide himself a lamb *for a burnt offering*" (Genesis 22:7). He did so in the person of our Lord; and the Lord chose willingly to dedicate himself to his Father's work every day continually. He became the great example for all who try to follow him. Our dedication

57

can never match his, just as the burnt offerings brought by individual Israelites were completely consumed while the nation's burnt offering continued to ascend acceptably before God.

The other difference between the burnt offering for the nation, and those brought by individuals, was that trumpets were blown over the nation's sacrifice:

"In the day of your gladness, and in your solemn days, and in the beginnings of your months, ye shall blow with trumpets over your burnt offerings, and over the sacrifices of your peace offerings." (Numbers 10:10)

None of the men or women in Israel would want a trumpet to be blown when they made their burnt offerings, unless they sought "glory from men" (cp. Matthew 6:2). But it is very different when we acknowledge what the Lord achieved. It is as if, by the blowing of trumpets, God was calling special attention to His special lamb – the one who preeminently presented his body as a living sacrifice, holy and acceptable to God.

MAIN POINTS OF THE BURNT OFFERING

- A voluntary offering symbolising dedication
- Wholly burnt so that the offering would rise before God as a sweet savour: this represented the faithful commitment of the offerer
- The skin was removed because God is not concerned with the outward appearance
- The carcase was separated into parts for inspection and cleansing
- The inner parts and legs received special attention
- The parts were laid in order on the altar – head, fat, and flesh – representing the mind, heart and body of the offerer
- The daily, continual, burnt offering for the nation symbolised the unfailing dedication of the Lord Jesus Christ for his people

9

"LET US OFFER THE SACRIFICE OF PRAISE"
Leviticus 3:1-17; 7:11-34

ONLY after the sin offering, the trespass offering and the burnt offering were made could a peace offering be sacrificed: the last of the four main offerings. Like the burnt offering, which we have just considered, the peace offering was a voluntary offering, and Israelites were encouraged by God to bring it willingly.* Compared with other offerings that could be brought for sacrifice, the peace offering had two unique aspects: it is the only one that could be eaten by the common people; and it is the only one where the person making the offering could actually bring some of the sacrificial animal to the altar. The priests had their portions of the sin offering and trespass offering, and the burnt offering was wholly consumed on the altar; but by bringing a peace offering to the altar with his own hands an Israelite could sit down at God's table and share a meal with Him. There can hardly be a more eloquent expression of fellowship, which is the main lesson of the peace offering, and the details of the sacrifice help to explain important principles about the wonderful privilege of being in covenant relationship with God.

No one is completely certain how best to translate *shelamim*, the Hebrew word for peace offerings. Terms such as "shared-offering" (NEB); "fellowship offering" (NIV) and "communion offering" (Jerusalem Bible) are not strictly translations, but are based on the detailed features of the offering contained in the law. Scholars sometimes take the word to be based on the root word

---

* Though it remained true that the peace offering was always voluntary, during the wilderness wanderings every animal killed for food had to be brought as a peace offering (Leviticus 17:1-6). This requirement was revoked for practical reasons once the nation settled in Canaan (Deuteronomy 12:20-25).

shalem, meaning "complete", and refer to the offering as "the *concluding* sacrifice"; i.e., the one offered last of all the major offerings.* The same meaning could also refer to the worshipper identifying himself completely with God, thus making his offering a "covenant sacrifice". The idea of calling it a peace offering rests on a connection between *shelamim* and the Hebrew word *shalom*, "peace". Peace in the Jewish mind is much more than simply the absence of conflict; it means health, prosperity and acceptance by God, so the Jewish Tanakh translates *shelamim* as the "well-being offering".

A Shared Meal

The details of the peace offering emphasize the fact that the meal was to be shared. The fat was completely consumed by fire and rose up before God as a sweet smelling savour (Leviticus 3:3-5; 9-11; 14-16); the right thigh was given to the priest who served at the altar (this was called "the heave thigh"); the breast was for Aaron and his sons (called "the wave breast", 7:31-34); and the remainder of the animal was returned to the person who brought the offering. The meal could then be eaten with family and friends, "before the LORD your God, and ye shall rejoice in all that ye put your hand unto, ye and your households, wherein the LORD thy God hath blessed thee" (Deuteronomy 12:7).

Further to emphasize that the peace offering was a shared meal, the worshippers brought unleavened cakes made with oil, unleavened wafers anointed with oil and loaves of leavened bread (Leviticus 7:12,13).

By giving the right leg of the sacrifice to the priest serving at the altar, the priest was receiving the best cut of meat and the strongest part of the animal. It was a "*heave* thigh (or shoulder)", so called from the Hebrew word meaning "to lift up" or "exalt". By serving at the altar, sometimes called 'God's table', the priest stood in God's place, and the person bringing the offering was intended to recognize his need to devote all his physical powers to God. The message of "the wave breast" was slightly different: this portion of the sacrifice was given to

---

* R E Clements, *Leviticus*, London 1970, page 14.

all the priests. The person bringing this offering acknowledged that he could not approach God without the presence of a priest to mediate on his behalf. The priests' mediatorial role was emphasized when Aaron and his sons were consecrated; the sacrifices that were offered during this ceremony were wave offerings because this is what the priests themselves were expected to be – their work was all undertaken openly before God.

"His own hands shall bring ..."

Apart from the peace offering being the only one that the person bringing the offering could eat, it was also different from all the others in that he was able to bring his sacrifice right to the altar: "his own hands shall bring the offerings of the LORD made by fire, the fat with the breast, it shall he bring, that the breast may be waved for a wave offering before the LORD" (Leviticus 7:30). The inward fat (Hebrew, *cheleb*) represented the choicest part of the animal, and comes to stand for "the best" part of any commodity (see Numbers 18:12,29,30,32). This fat was God's portion, and as Israelites carried it to the altar to offer it to Him they were acknowledging their own desire to offer the best of their lives in His service: their inward convictions and motivations.

What happened to the fat when it was brought to the altar? No special detail is included in the priestly instructions regarding the peace offering. Instead, there is just a passing comment when the burnt offering is described:

> "The fire upon the altar shall be kept burning thereon, it shall not go out; and the priest ... shall lay the burnt offering in order upon it, and shall burn thereon the fat of the peace offerings."
>
> (Leviticus 6:12, RV)

This relates to "the continual (daily) burnt offering", where two lambs were offered, one at the beginning and the other at the end of every day. The priest was to place the fat of the peace offerings upon this slowly consuming sacrifice. We concluded when looking at the burnt offering, that the daily burnt offering represented the complete dedication of the life of our Lord, so by placing the fat of the peace offering upon this special burnt offering, we are shown that the best things of our lives should be devoted to God on the basis of what the Lord Jesus Christ has achieved on our behalf.

"By him … continually"

The Apostle picks up this idea in the letter to the Hebrews, which is always so helpful in describing the intentions underlying the regulations given to Israel through Moses. After mentioning the special feature of the sin offering, "whose blood is brought into the holy place by the high priest as an offering for sin" (Hebrews 13:11, RV), the Apostle explains the response of those who have been redeemed by the blood of Christ:

"By him therefore let us offer the sacrifice of praise to God continually, that is, the fruit of our lips giving thanks to his name." (verse 15)

By explaining that our praise and thanksgiving have to be offered "continually … by (or through) him" – that is Jesus – it is apparent that the Apostle was inspired to see the true intention and meaning of the peace offering. Jesus continually, day by day without fail, committed himself to his Father's will; so we must continually thank God for His abundant mercies towards us.

Fellowship with God therefore involves and is expressed in praise and thanksgiving, and we should expect to find these factors featuring strongly in the details of the peace offerings that were given under the law.

Because peace offerings were not mandatory, various circumstances could encourage Israelites to bring them. They could bring a peace offering:

- to express thanksgiving – to commemorate deliverance from sickness or danger;
- in fulfilment of a vow – after promising to bring an offering to God for deliverance from distress;
- or purely as a freewill offering – when God's great mercies were acknowledged.

Depending on the circumstances that led to the offering being presented before God, the resulting meal had to be eaten within a specific time period: a thanksgiving offering had to be eaten the same day it was offered, whereas in the case of vows and freewill offerings, the meal could be consumed over two days. In every case, however, any meat left over – i.e., until the third day – was to be totally burnt because it was regarded as unclean (Leviticus 7:15-19). Equally, those who shared in the sacrificial meal had to be ritually clean, for "the soul that eateth of the flesh of the sacrifice of peace offerings, that pertain unto the Lord, having his uncleanness upon him, even that soul shall be cut off from his people" (verse 20).

The Prominence of Thanksgiving

There is obviously an order of importance in the three versions of the peace offering. The one that expressed thanksgiving was superior to the others because it could only be eaten on the day it was offered. Thanksgiving is therefore a vital aspect of worship and it plays an important part in fellowship, as we have already seen. The other two forms of peace offering had to be consumed within two days; but of these two offerings, the one connected with a vow is more important than the freewill offering. Unusually for offerings that were being sacrificed to God, the freewill peace offering could be less than physically perfect:

> "A bullock or a lamb that hath any thing superfluous or lacking in his parts, that mayest thou offer for a freewill offering; but for a vow it shall not be accepted."
> (Leviticus 22:23)

The importance of the thanksgiving offering is also apparent when the offerings are mentioned elsewhere in scripture. The Psalmist, for example, in Psalm 50 concludes that, "whoso offereth praise (Hebrew, *towdah*, a thanksgiving sacrifice) glorifieth me: and to him that ordereth his conversation aright will I shew the salvation of God" (Psalm 50:23). This lovely Hebrew parallelism shows how a properly ordered life will result in thanksgiving, and how God promises to respond as the Saviour of those who seek to glorify His name. Earlier in the same Psalm there is another reference to the importance of the peace offering. God says –

> "Will I eat the flesh of bulls, or drink the blood of goats? Offer unto God thanksgiving (*towdah*); and pay thy vows unto the most High: and call upon me in the

day of trouble: I will deliver thee, and thou shalt glorify me." (verses 13-15)

This explains some of the circumstances that would cause the Israelites to bring their peace offerings. True thanksgiving will be shown by a determination to keep any promise that is made to God, and He will recognise the true and devoted heart by showing divine deliverance in the day of trouble.*

No Barrier in God's Plan of Salvation

Offerings like this – to express thanksgiving, to remember a solemn vow, or ones offered in a spontaneous acknowledgement of God's mercy – could be made by anyone in Israel; and the animals they were allowed to bring emphasized the universal nature of the peace offering. Almost invariably, only male animals were allowed for the other three offerings: sin,** trespass and burnt offerings. But because the peace offering expresses the principles of fellowship within the covenant, male and female animals were allowed, expressing the absence of any human barrier in God's plan of salvation.

Together with the fact that some blemished animals could be sacrificed as peace offerings, and that the meal was accompanied by leavened and unleavened food, these details explain that God has never offered true fellowship on the basis of human righteousness. The animals that were brought as peace offerings were like the people who brought them: some were male, some female; some were complete in all their parts, others were halt, lame or blind. But God was showing His people how the message of salvation is for all people, on the basis of an acceptable sacrifice – the Lamb without blemish.

This was portrayed in a very beautiful way by the association of peace offerings with the Feast of Pentecost. Pentecost was the only feast in the religious calendar where peace offerings were required: "two he-lambs of the

---

* Similar connections between offering thanksgiving and paying vows can be found in other passages too, such as Psalm 116:17,18 and Jonah 2:9.
** Female animals were, however, required for the sin offerings brought by the common people.

first year for a sacrifice of peace offerings" (Leviticus 23:19, RV). By relating the schedule of feasts to the work of the Lord Jesus Christ, we can see how Passover was fulfilled in his death; and how in his resurrection he became the "firstfruits of them that slept" (1 Corinthians 15:20), as represented by waving the first sheaf of the harvest before the Lord. Fifty days later, when Pentecost was celebrated, two wave loaves foretold that both Jews and Gentiles would be saved; and the bringing also of two he-lambs as peace offerings further emphasized the extent of the salvation offered to mankind through the work of Christ.

Acts 2:1 therefore says, "When the day of Pentecost was *fully* come", or fulfilled, the Gospel was preached to a multitude "out of every nation under heaven", and "about three thousand souls" were baptized, forming the first ecclesia of the new covenant in Christ. These three thousand joined with the Lord's apostles, in their "doctrine and fellowship, and in breaking of bread, and in prayers" (verses 5,41,42).

In this time of new beginning, a multitude that formed the nucleus of the new people of God began to offer the sacrifice of praise to God continually. If we learn the lesson of the peace offering, the fruit of our lips should combine with theirs in giving thanks to His name.

MAIN POINTS OF THE PEACE OFFERING

- A voluntary offering symbolising thanksgiving, covenant relationship and fellowship with God
- Closely associated with the Feast of Pentecost
- Offered in thanksgiving for deliverance, in fulfilment of a vow, or in spontaneous worship
- The only sacrifice that could be eaten by the worshipper – a shared meal with God
- Male and female animals were allowed, including some with imperfections; also leavened and unleavened food, because God's salvation is for all people
- Could only be eaten by those who were ritually clean
- The meal could not be left until the third day, to prevent corruption
- The offerer brought the sacrifice right up to the altar; he had access to God's table
- The inner fat, representing the choicest and best, was placed on top of the daily burnt offering, showing how our best service to God is wholly dependent on the work of Christ
- The animal's right leg was given to the officiating priest, indicating that our physical powers should always be devoted to God
- The animal's breast was given to all the priests, acknowledging man's need for priestly mediation

10

MY MEAT IS TO DO HIS WILL
Leviticus 2:1-16; 6:14-18

ALMOST all the offerings discussed so far involved the sacrifice of animals, emphasising the importance of blood shedding before sinful man can enter acceptably into relationship with God. But one offering was completely free from blood shedding: the meal offering.* This offering could be brought alone, but was more usually associated with burnt offerings and peace offerings, for neither of these could be sacrificed without an accompanying meal offering.** In these cases, the quantity of meal related to the size of animal being offered, and a drink offering was also made (Numbers 15:1-15).

Burnt / Peace Offering	Meal Offering	Drink Offering
For each lamb	⅒ ephah of fine flour, ¼ hin of oil	¼ hin of wine
For each ram	²⁄₁₀ ephah of fine flour, ⅓ hin of oil	⅓ hin of wine
For each bullock	³⁄₁₀ ephah of fine flour, ½ hin of oil	½ hin of wine

The word translated "meal offering" (Hebrew, *minchah*) literally means a 'present' or a 'gift', and is sometimes used to describe the tribute paid by a conquered people (e.g., 2 Chronicles 17:11). By bringing a meal offering, the Israelites acknowledged God's supreme sovereignty. As a

---

* Unfortunately referred to in KJV as the meat offering; but here meat = food. Other translations call it the grain (NIV) or cereal (RSV) offering.
** Details of the meal offering therefore appear in Leviticus 2 between those for burnt offerings (chapter 1) and peace offerings (chapter 3).

'gift' or a 'present', the meal offering was voluntary, and was brought to God out of the abundance of a man's heart. A notable occasion occurred when Israel first harvested the fruits of the land; Moses encouraged the people to take these first fruits to the priest, saying: "I have brought the firstfruits of the land, which thou, O LORD, hast given me" (Deuteronomy 26:10). The Israelites thereby acknowledged that all they had came from God.

The meal offering could take various forms: it could be baked in an oven or fried in a pan as loaves or cakes. The ingredients were to be the finest flour mixed only with oil: no leaven was allowed because part of the offering was burnt on the altar, and neither leaven nor honey could be burnt. Only a portion – just a handful – was placed on the altar, as a "memorial". The priests ate the remainder, because the offering was holy: sanctified through being brought and offered to God as He directed (Leviticus 2:9,10).

Sin Offering for the Poor

We have noted that *almost* all other offerings were of animals. The exception was the sin offering for the poorest in the land. If a person could not bring a lamb or goat, God allowed two pigeons or turtle doves in their place; and if an Israelite was too poor to bring two pigeons, he could bring an offering of fine flour. On the surface it seems as if this sin offering was the same as the meal offering, but a closer consideration reveals important differences (see table below).

Sin offering for the poor (5:11-13)	Meal offering (2:1-16; 6:14-18; Numbers 28:5)
⅒ ephah of fine flour	⅒ ephah of fine flour
No oil allowed	Oil was necessary
No frankincense allowed	Frankincense was necessary
A handful burned as a memorial	A handful burned as a memorial
Remainder was for the priests	Remainder was for the priests

The sin offering was never intended to be a sweet savour before God. Sin can never be pleasing to Him, so the sin offering was not mixed with oil or garnished with frankincense. This also explains why the meal offering never accompanied either the sin offering or the trespass offering: it was inappropriate for any man or woman to commemorate sins and transgressions.

Jealousy Offering

Another offering related to the sin offering for the poor was brought when a man suspected his wife's unfaithfulness (Numbers 5:11-31). This "jealousy offering" was a tenth of an ephah of barley meal (not fine flour) without oil or frankincense. The memorial handful was first placed in the woman's hands, and when she protested her innocence it was waved before God and then burned on the altar.

Some other offerings are also similar to the meal offering. There was the priest's offering, for example, presented to God "in the day when he is anointed" (Leviticus 6:20). A tenth of an ephah of fine flour was baked with oil and brought to the altar. It was different from the meal offering in that it was "wholly burnt: it shall not be eaten" (verse 23). Half was offered in the morning, and half in the evening, perpetually. It was therefore like the continual, daily burnt offering and expressed how the priest's work was intended always to rise up before God.

A further connection with the meal offering makes a leading part of its intended teaching absolutely plain. In all the cases that have been considered, the amount of offering brought before God was a tenth of an ephah. This amount is first recorded in connection with God's provision of manna in the wilderness, where an omer of manna was sufficient to provide food for an individual Israelite for one day. Exodus 16 concludes by explaining: "now an omer is the tenth part of an ephah" (Exodus 16:36). This amount of food, sufficient to sustain a person for one day, clearly represents a single man or woman in Israel.

The Shewbread

In a later chapter in Leviticus details are given about the shewbread in the tabernacle, which take the information about the meal offering and extends it from the individual in Israel to the nation as a whole. Twelve loaves were prepared: a loaf for each tribe, made from fine flour. The amount of flour in each loaf was two tenth parts of an ephah, possibly representing the males and females of each tribe. Pure frankincense was put on the loaves as a memorial, and the loaves were constantly before God, replaced by a new baking each Sabbath day. When the previous week's loaves were removed they were eaten by the priests in a holy place (Leviticus 24:5-9).

Closely related to the shewbread were the offerings made at the time of first-fruits and Pentecost. At first-fruits there was a meal offering of "two tenth parts of an ephah of fine flour" (Leviticus 23:13); and at Pentecost two loaves were produced, baked with leaven, each comprising "two tenth parts of an ephah". They are described as "a new meal offering unto the LORD" (verse16). The two Pentecost loaves were waved before the Lord, not this time representing the tribes of Israel; but one loaf stood for Jews and the other for Gentiles who will comprise the harvest at the end of the age (Matthew 13:39).

The Result of Labour

The emphasis on a tenth of an ephah, mainly of fine flour, in all these related offerings points strongly to the individual Israelite and his works. He had to bring the offering himself, and it had to be carefully prepared. It was not simply a sheaf of corn, but corn that had been threshed, winnowed and ground. The fine flour was also mixed with oil and cooked. With regard to the 'memorial portion' of the offering, frankincense that had been beaten small was placed on it; and wine made from harvested, trodden, and fermented grapes was poured over it. Even when the meal offering was of the first-fruits, it had to be "green ears of corn dried by the fire, even corn beaten out of full ears" (Leviticus 2:14). The preparation of the meal offering involved the work of human hands. In this respect it was different from the animals brought for sacrifice, which had only been fed and tended by man. The meal offering therefore taught two important lessons:

- it represented the individual who brought it (a tenth of an ephah was equivalent to one day's food supply);

- because of the careful preparation required, the meal offering also represented a person's labours.

When a sin offering was brought in the form of fine flour, it denoted a person's transgressions, and thanks and joy have no part in iniquity. So the sin offering and the jealousy offering were alike free from oil and frankincense. But the priest's offering and the meal offering represented man's labours in God's service; they revealed that devotions should be made towards Him, and thus meal offerings were fittingly associated with burnt offerings and peace offerings – with devotion and fellowship.

In order to be acceptable before God, a man's labours need to comply with God's requirements. He asked that meal offerings be mixed with oil, teaching that human labours should be assisted by the application of God's word, and undertaken with joy and gladness in acknowledgement of His purpose. By placing frankincense on the offering,* this was clearly pointing to the need for our daily activities to be offered before God in a prayerful manner, recognising that they are ultimately for His glory.

Every Sacrifice shall be Salted

God's acceptance of man's labours, when presented before Him in the manner set out in the law, was shown by the burning of a memorial handful of the offering. The priests ate the remainder as His representatives; they also had to eat the offering in "a holy place". Yet how can man present anything to God acceptably? This was a question many godly men and women thought about deeply, and there was another ingredient involved in the sacrifice that provides an answer; for only through being the people of God were Israelites able to offer their service to Him:

> "Every oblation of thy meal offering shalt thou season with salt; neither shalt thou suffer the salt of the covenant of thy God to be lacking from thy meal offering: with all thine offerings thou shalt offer salt."
>
> (Leviticus 2:13)

---

* All the frankincense was burnt with the memorial portion (Leviticus 2:2,16). Frankincense was for burning, not for eating.

There was a practical reason for adding salt, as it would aid the burning of the portion offered on the altar, and season the remainder eaten by the priests. But the spiritual lessons were far more significant. Honey and leaven were completely excluded because they assist fermentation and hence corruption. Salt acts differently: it helps prevent corruption as well as making a meal more palatable. Salt therefore expresses permanence, especially when it is related to God's covenant with Israel. Both these aspects have their spiritual counterparts. A "covenant of salt" is another way of describing the fellowship of a shared meal, and to "have salt in yourselves" is another way of saying, "have peace one with another" (Mark 9:50). Jesus based this teaching on Leviticus 2:13, which he summarised as follows: "Every one shall be salted with fire, and every sacrifice shall be salted with salt" (verse 49).

In making this connection, Jesus was showing some aspects of the meal offering that are still applicable to his disciples, and the Apostle Paul further takes up the idea in his letters to Colosse and Ephesus. The meal offering represented the outcome of a dedicated life, shown in Christ-like behaviour: "Let your speech be alway with grace, seasoned with salt, that ye may know how ye ought to answer every man" (Colossians 4:6). And, lest we are left in any doubt about his meaning, he wrote to the Ephesians, "Let no corrupt communication proceed out of your mouth, but that which is good to the use of edifying, that it may minister grace unto the hearers" (Ephesians 4:29).

"He poured out his soul"

By the association of meal offerings with burnt offerings and peace offerings, anyone bringing a meal offering was showing that acceptable service in God's sight arises from commitment and dedication to His ways, and through the fellowship created by the forgiveness of sins. The grounds for fellowship with God were further emphasised by pouring a drink offering over the meal offering. All the drink offering of "strong drink" (Numbers 28:7) was poured out on the altar; it did not form part of the meal eaten by the priests as wine was forbidden to them while on duty before the Lord God (Leviticus 10:9-11).

Without the accompanying drink offering, it is possible that the real message of the meal offering would pass us by. As we have concluded, the meal offering represented men's labours when they are dedicated to God. We have also seen how faithful Israelites would question their right to present their frail and inconclusive service to Him. But there was one who was able to say: "My meat is to do the will of him that sent me, and to finish his work" (John 4:34). The Lord Jesus' work was seen in its most complete form when he laid down his life so that we might be saved; and we acknowledge this on each occasion we take bread and wine in memory of him. He "poured out his soul unto death" (Isaiah 53:12). The meal and drink offerings were Old Testament precursors of the bread and wine. We partake of that feast in the knowledge that Jesus has promised to eat and drink anew in his Father's kingdom.

The Lord Jesus thus provides the pattern we must follow; his self-sacrificial life of service became the model for all his disciples. The Apostle Paul was one who practised the Master's methods. He wrote to the Philippians about his work on their behalf: "Yes, and if I be offered (i.e., poured out as a drink offering, RV margin) upon the sacrifice and service of your faith, I joy, and rejoice with you all" (Philippians 2:17). To become better disciples of the Lord, we should learn the lesson of the meal offering: to make it our meat to do the will of God at all times; and to be so concerned with the needs of our fellow disciples to pour ourselves out completely for their sakes.

MAIN POINTS OF THE MEAL OFFERING

- A voluntary offering symbolising works of righteousness and joy that flow from being at peace with God and dedicated to His service
- Always offered with burnt offerings and peace offerings, but never with sin offerings and trespass offerings
- Comprised a tenth of an ephah of fine flour – one day's food – representing each individual
- Mixed with oil to show that man's joyful labour must always be directed by God's word
- No leaven or honey were allowed, as these are agents of corruption, and to indicate God's eternal covenant
- Salt had to be added to prevent corruption and for seasoning
- One handful was burnt on the altar with frankincense and a drink offering
- The remainder was eaten by the priests in a holy place
- Jesus fulfilled the object of the meal and drink offerings when he followed perfectly his Father's will, and sought always to do His work

11

"CONSIDER THE APOSTLE AND HIGH PRIEST"
Leviticus 8,9

ANY Israelite reading the details of the law of sacrifice contained in the opening chapters of Leviticus would soon realise that he could do nothing without a priest. While part of the message informed him about his personal responsibilities – what animals to bring, and how they should be prepared and sacrificed (Leviticus 1–5) – there followed a section specifically for the priests, explaining their responsibilities and duties (chapters 6,7). The message could not be clearer: no individual in Israel could draw near to God without either a sacrifice or a priest. Furthermore, the importance of the priests is emphasised again by the next section of the book, which looks at the inauguration of the priesthood (chapters 8–10).

A Kingdom of Priests

When Israel left Egypt, and as they prepared for the day when God would descend on Mount Sinai, He told them that they would be "a kingdom of priests, and an holy nation" (Exodus 19:6). It becomes apparent from what follows that this intention could not be fully realised while sin and death continued to reign on the earth: their role as priests was therefore a future hope, not a present reality. Yet in His mercy God provided priests from their own ranks to manifest through form and ritual what He was seeking voluntarily from each individual in the nation. Only a priestly nation was allowed to approach before God, and He provided a priestly family to aid the nation's approach. Israel was being shown that no individual was truly fit to stand before God; yet in the arrangements involving the priests the nation was also being shown an acted parable about the holiness God seeks in His people.

This important message was presented to Israel through the principle of representation: a principle that underpins much of the law. They were called to be a holy people and a kingdom of priests, so when priests were inaugurated they represented the nation as a whole. Therefore when Moses was instructed to take Aaron and his sons to appoint them as priests, the whole congregation was also called together to the door of the tabernacle (Leviticus 8:3). They were to witness all that happened, recognising that it was undertaken on their behalf and for their benefit. Symbolically, it also showed God's requirements for all who seek to approach Him. This is no better expressed than by the Apostle in the Letter to the Hebrews:

"For every high priest taken from among men is ordained for men in things pertaining to God, that he may offer both gifts and sacrifices for sins: who can have compassion on the ignorant, and on them that are out of the way; for that he himself also is compassed with infirmity." (Hebrews 5:1,2)

Called of God

Yet even the priest himself was only representative of one still greater who was to come. The quality that fitted him to be a sympathetic and compassionate priest also disqualified him from claiming the right of priesthood: he had, "as for the people, so also for himself, to offer for sins. And no man taketh this honour unto himself, but he that is called of God" (verse 3).

Notice in the above passage the verbal connection with Hebrews 2:14 – "he himself also" – another passage which makes the same point: that the Lord shared the same nature as those he came to save, leading to another declaration about Jesus' role as priest:

"Wherefore in all points it behoved him (Jesus) to be made like unto his brethren, that he might be a merciful and faithful high priest in things pertaining to God, to make reconciliation for the sins of the people." (Hebrews 2:17)

Through God's choice, therefore, and by means of His provision, Aaron and his sons were appointed as priests. Ritually and symbolically they were made fit to act not only as representatives of the people, but more importantly as representative of the great intercessor God would provide to make reconciliation for sinful men and women. The role of the priesthood had already been declared in Exodus:

"There (i.e., in the tabernacle) I will meet with the children of Israel, and the tabernacle shall be sanctified by my glory. And I will sanctify the tabernacle of the congregation, and the altar: I will sanctify also both Aaron and his sons, to minister to me in the priest's office. And I will dwell among the children of Israel, and will be their God." (Exodus 29:43-45)

This promise relating to Aaron and his sons was fulfilled by the events recorded in Leviticus 8, and it is possible to place these alongside the details in Exodus 29 to see how God's commands were faithfully put into practice once the tabernacle was erected and ready for use.

National Crisis

But there was a serious crisis in Israel between the declaration in Exodus 29 and the actual inauguration of the priests as recorded in Leviticus 8. While Moses was in the mount receiving God's commands, Aaron was persuaded by the people to make the golden calf, and he stood by while they worshipped the work of men's hands and committed all sorts of abominations in God's sight, so that He determined to destroy them. Moses was desperately concerned about God's reaction, and pleaded with Him. Moses did not wish to presume on God's mercy, yet prayed earnestly that He would forgive their sin (Exodus 32:32).

The seriousness of the nation's sin in the matter of the golden calf showed graphically how sin separates between man and God, and man's desperate need for atonement. God's response was to provide in the midst of the nation a constant reminder of His presence and His holiness, and to establish a process whereby the nation could regularly obtain forgiveness and reconciliation. These were the functions of the tabernacle, of the schedule of sacrifices, and of the priesthood. The inauguration of the priesthood was therefore a fundamental part of God's response to the nation's sin.

The amazing aspect, however, is that the family chosen to act as representatives of, and on behalf of the nation

77

was Aaron's! While Aaron did not personally instigate the worship of the golden calf, he certainly took a leading part in assisting those who called on him to make gods to worship like the ones they had known in Egypt. Aaron, in common with the rest of the nation, was spared from God's wrath only by the intervention of Moses, who interceded on their behalf.

After that intercession, and a further ascent of Sinai to receive the second set of tables containing the commandments, Moses returned with the message that the tabernacle was to be constructed exactly as previously described (cp. Exodus 35–39 and 25–30). Work on the tabernacle was accompanied by work on priestly garments, but without any certainty as to who would undertake that important office and wear the priest's clothes. The last chapter of Exodus records the events of the first day of the first month of Israel's second year after leaving Egypt. It was the day the Tabernacle was erected, by the hand and under the leadership of Moses. Neither Aaron nor his sons played any part in the erection or dedication of the tabernacle.

Moses' Role as Priest

As the book of Exodus ends, we are left in suspense. Will Aaron be appointed high priest, or did his involvement with the golden calf forever disbar him from priestly duties? Leviticus 8 removes all doubt. Aaron was to be restored, despite the shame of that sordid affair, showing that in God's mercy even a sinner like Aaron can be appointed to such a high office.* But though attention now focuses on Aaron and his sons, we must not lose sight of his younger brother Moses. Throughout, Moses has a central role. He mediates between God and the priests, just as the priest's role was to be that of a mediator between God and the nation. Before ever there was an Aaronic priesthood, Moses acted as priest.

Moses played an important part in Aaron's ordination. Moses conducted the ceremony; Moses shared in the sacrifices, where normally this was restricted to the

---

* Is there a parallel in Peter retaining his position among the Apostles after three times denying his Lord?

priests alone; Moses, not the priests, received the wave breast; Moses sprinkled the anointing oil. Moses was undoubtedly representing God on this occasion, as so often throughout his life. The writer to Hebrews explains how this representation was of the nature of a servant for his Lord, "Moses verily was faithful in all his (God's) house, as a servant" (Hebrews 3:5). Wonderful though this was, the Apostle reminds his readers that the Lord Jesus Christ was faithful, not as a servant, but as a Son. Moses was engaged in testifying to "things which were to be spoken after"; he pointed forward to a greater reality. If Moses was superior to Aaron the high priest, what could be said of Christ?

Attention now passes from Moses to Aaron and his sons; they came to the tabernacle in the sight of all the people who were present to witness the inauguration of Aaron's family as priests. Leviticus 8 records the details of that week-long ceremony, where Moses undertook all the priestly duties. Once Aaron and his sons were consecrated, they were able to act as priests.

The Inauguration Ceremony

The inauguration ceremony lasted seven days, beginning with Aaron and his sons washing themselves completely in water from the laver (Leviticus 8:6). This was the start of a process of ritual cleansing, separation and consecration. Aaron was clothed in the high priestly garments, which were completed by fixing the golden plate over his forehead, saying "Holiness to the LORD" (verses 7-9). This was the objective of all that followed: to bind Aaron to God's service, and to separate him to the priest's work. Taking the anointing oil, Moses dedicated the tabernacle, the altar and its vessels, and finally Aaron himself (verses 10-12).

Anointing oil was poured liberally over Aaron's head: he represented the nation and was to act as its spiritual head; and in turn he was represented by his head. As the anointing oil flowed down from his head, over his beard and even to the skirt of his priestly garments, the whole nation was being representatively anointed, and encouraged to "dwell together in unity" (Psalm 133:1,2). Aaron's sons were also clothed in priestly garments, so that they could join with their father when a bullock was slain as a sin offering. As priests they were to be separated from sin so that they could dedicate themselves wholly and completely to their appointed task. After the sin offering was presented, a ram was prepared and sacrificed as a burnt offering, before a second ram was offered. This second ram was called "the ram of consecration" (Leviticus 8:22, cp. Exodus 29:19,20). Essentially, it was a peace offering expressing the priests' joy and delight at entering into God's service, and acknowledging the fellowship He had invited them to share with Him. The blood of this ram was placed on the tip of their right ears, the thumb of their right hands, and the big toe of their right feet.

The principle of representation is once again apparent in this ceremony. In scripture, the right side stands for favour and blessing (e.g., Genesis 48:17), the ear for hearing, the hands for doing, and the feet for walking. God's intention for the priests was that they should have holy ears to hear His word, holy hands to do His service, and holy feet to walk always in His ways.

A Fellowship Meal

There were portions of the consecration offering, as with all peace offerings, that the priests could eat. Aaron and his sons shared this meal within the tabernacle precincts: a meal of meat from the ram, and loaves and cakes that had been brought as an accompanying meal offering (Leviticus 8:31). As the inauguration ceremony lasted seven days, these offerings were repeated throughout the week, and the priests had to remain – on pain of death – "at the door of the tabernacle" for the whole time, showing the need for devotion to their future work (verses 33-35).

As all this happened in the sight of the whole congregation, it reinforced what was implicit in the arrangements for the offerings, that no one in Israel could approach God without the services of an anointed priest.

After the inaugural week, Aaron and his sons took over as priests and they were able to officiate on behalf of the nation and individuals. The importance of their office was established by a singular comment from Moses: "This is the thing which the LORD commanded that ye should do: and the glory of the LORD shall appear unto you"

(Leviticus 9:6). By virtue of their intermediary work, God would reveal Himself to the people in glory. It is impossible to read Moses' words without considering "the Apostle and High Priest of our profession, Christ Jesus" (Hebrews 3:1), through whom God reveals Himself to us in glory (2 Corinthians 4:6). But before the priests could officiate for their brethren, their personal position had to be recognised. The drawback of the Aaronic priesthood was that "every high priest taken from among men ... is compassed with infirmity. And by reason hereof he ought, as for the people, so for himself, to offer for sins" (Hebrews 5:1-3). It was possible that, despite the sanctification provided during the week-long inauguration ceremony, and despite the new priests' unbroken residence in the tabernacle precincts, some defect had occurred because of their infirmity. Their first task was to offer a sin offering and a burnt offering. On all subsequent occasions the sin offering for the priest and for the nation was to be a bullock (Leviticus 4:3,13,14), but not this time.

Aaron was told to take "*a young calf* for a sin offering" for himself (9:2). There was special significance in Aaron's offering being a calf of the first year, for had he not – early in the first year of their coming out of Egypt – taken the people's gold and fashioned it into a molten calf (Exodus 32:4)?

The Priestly Blessing

A ram for a burnt offering followed, representing the dedication God requires of those who seek to serve Him, and the priests' dedication was immediately put into practice as offerings were made on behalf of all the people (Leviticus 9:12-21). As Aaron came down from making these offerings on the altar, he "lifted up his hand toward the people, and blessed them" (verse 22). This was the priestly blessing recorded in Numbers:

> "The LORD bless thee, and keep thee: the LORD make his face shine upon thee, and be gracious unto thee: the LORD lift up his countenance upon thee, and give thee peace." (Numbers 6:24-27)

Then, and only then, as Aaron and Moses came out of the tabernacle, did God's glory appear:

"The glory of the LORD appeared unto all the people. And there came a fire out from before the LORD, and consumed upon the altar the burnt offering and the fat: which when all the people saw, they shouted and fell on their faces." (Leviticus 9:23,24)

Through the work of the priesthood, Israel was once again reconciled to God. He blessed them and showed them His glory, and accepted their work and their praise. If this was true for Israel, and with priests who were "compassed with infirmity", how much more must it be true for those whose priest "became the author of salvation to all them that obey him" (Hebrews 5:9).

SUMMARY OF THE PRIESTS' INAUGURATION

- the priests represented the holy nation, called to be "a kingdom of priests"; they also manifested the need for an effective priest – the Lord Jesus Christ
- the inauguration involved ritual washing, and putting on dedicated clothing to show their "Holiness to the Lord", as the golden plate on Aaron's turban declared
- Aaron's head was liberally anointed with oil, which flowed down his garments to show the joy of national unity
- three sacrifices were offered – a bullock for a sin offering, a ram for a burnt offering and a ram for a peace offering. Blood from the peace offering was placed on each priest's right ear, thumb and big toe, showing their dedication to God's word in mind, act and walk
- it was possible that the priests may sin, even during the inaugural week in the tabernacle court, and they therefore offered a sin offering. On this occasion it was to be a young calf, perhaps to remind Aaron of his involvement in the incident of the golden calf
- at the end of the ceremony, Aaron recited the priestly blessing upon the people, and God's fiery glory appeared before them all, totally consuming the offerings

12

PRIESTS WITH INFIRMITY
Leviticus 10

WHEN Aaron and his sons were inaugurated as priests, "the glory of the LORD appeared" in fire, indicating God's acceptance of those who were consecrated. The divine approval was seen in the glory and the fire. The detailed instructions about sacrifices in the first seven chapters of Leviticus showed the need for priests to mediate between the people and God, and now priests were available to minister before the Lord.

Yet, as the Apostle wrote to Hebrew believers many centuries later, "the law appointeth men high priests, *having infirmity*" (Hebrews 7:28, RV). In the midst of the obvious celebrations that attended the priestly consecration ceremony, the incident recorded in Leviticus 10 sounds a jarring note. The fire that so shortly before had consumed the burnt offering and that conveyed God's pleasure now smote two of Aaron's sons in an act that showed His severe displeasure: the fire of blessing became a fire of judgement. The incident, occurring so early in the life of the ecclesia in the wilderness foreshadowed a similar turn of events in the early days of the New Testament ecclesia, when Ananias and Sapphira died at God's hand for disobeying His word (Acts 5:1-11).

Defiant and Presumptuous
In both cases, the misdemeanour followed quickly upon a time of great rejoicing: in the Old Testament incident, almost certainly on the same day that God's glory appeared before the people.* This leads us to enquire what caused Aaron's sons, Nadab and Abihu, to act so disastrously, and so shortly after their consecration? Seven days had been spent in the tabernacle courts during

---

* See Leviticus 10:19, which states that the incident occurred on the day the special sin and burnt offerings were presented – i.e., the eighth day of the ceremony of consecration (see 9:8,12).

the consecration ceremony, yet the two new priests quickly did things which God "commanded them not" (Leviticus 10:1). There can be no doubt that their actions were defiant and presumptuous, and that God's response was just. The incident has been recorded as a warning, requiring us to consider carefully the factors that were involved.

Leviticus 10 departs from the pattern established in chapters 8 and 9. Chapter 8 records God's commands to Moses, which were faithfully passed on to Aaron: "Moses did as the LORD commanded him" (8:4). Chapter 9 therefore confirms for Aaron "the thing which the LORD commanded that ye should do" (9:6). But there are no similar phrases in chapter 10. Nadab and Abihu act on their own initiative, and not at all in accordance with God's commands. Though the outcome was disastrous for them, their failure to follow God's word gives greater emphasis to God's instructions to His servants.

Nadab and Abihu are first mentioned in connection with an earlier account, when they accompanied Moses, Aaron, Joshua and the seventy elders of Israel who ascended Mount Sinai to see the God of Israel enthroned in glory (Exodus 24:1-11). Though only Moses and Joshua drew near to God on that occasion, it was an enormous privilege for Aaron's sons to be involved.* Yet it is possible that, even so, Nadab and Abihu were envious of Moses' leadership. Later in the wilderness journey, Korah, Dathan and Abiram challenged Moses' leadership because of envy, and it would not be surprising if his nephews felt even more strongly that their position should be more privileged, for was not their father older than their uncle Moses? Yet when the elders of Israel went up Sinai, God said, "*Moses alone* shall come near the LORD: but they shall not come nigh" (verse 2).

---

* Aaron and his wife Elisheba had four sons (Exodus 6:23). Perhaps Eleazar and Ithamar were too young to be part of the company that ascended Sinai. Nadab and Abihu were both young men, perhaps still in their early twenties in Leviticus 10, for they died childless (1 Chronicles 24:2).

Exceeding their Office

Their challenge was not only against Moses, with whom the Lord spake "face to face, as a man speaketh unto his friend" (Exodus 33:11), but also against Aaron, for his sons "took either of them his censer", thus assuming a *high* priestly role. It is therefore possible that their sin occurred not through envy alone, but because their hearts were lifted up through pride as a result of being sons of the high priest. Leviticus 16:12,13 explains how the high priest was to take incense as he went in before God on the annual Day of Atonement, so Nadab and Abihu "drew near before the LORD" (verse 1, RV), presumably by seeking to enter the most holy place, and they died "before the sanctuary" (10:4). Even if they were not anticipating the high priest's work on the Day of Atonement, Exodus 30:7-9 makes the high priest responsible for offering incense with the morning and evening sacrifices. Furthermore, he was specifically told not to offer any "strange incense" (verse 9), presumably incense that was not compounded in accordance with God's specific directions.

Leviticus 10, however, speaks not of strange incense but of "strange fire", without explaining just what this means. The incense should have been burnt using coals from the altar of burnt offering, and Nadab and Abihu may have used some other alternative. Yet the fire is not described as "strange" earlier in the verse, suggesting that the whole action was wrong and unauthorised, and that one or more of the following was totally unacceptable in God's sight:

- wrong censers were used;
- the incense was not properly prepared;
- the fire did not come from the altar of burnt offering;
- Nadab and Abihu were not authorised to offer incense at that time;
- they tried to enter the most holy place, which was forbidden to them;
- they were not in the right frame of mind to undertake the duty.

This last possibility has attracted attention because, after explaining how the men's bodies were to be removed, God forbad all priests in the future from partaking of alcohol when on priestly duty (Leviticus 10:9). Were Nadab and Abihu drunk on duty, and therefore not able properly to discriminate the details of God's commands concerning incense?*

However it came about, their behaviour was utterly offensive to God, who proclaimed His displeasure to Aaron: "I will be sanctified in them that come nigh me, and before all the people I will be glorified" (Leviticus 10:3). When the people saw God's glory consume the sacrifice, they shouted for joy. Aaron, seeing the same fire take the lives of his sons, now "held his peace". God had spoken, and Aaron knew he could not plead mitigating circumstances. The message could hardly be clearer. If the people wished to rejoice again – if they wished to see God's glory – they and their priests must be sanctified. This call to holiness is the great theme of Leviticus: "without which no man shall see the Lord" (Hebrews 12:14). God responds to holiness by revealing His glory.

Defilement through Death

The week-long inauguration ceremony for the priests should have made it abundantly apparent how easily men and women can be defiled, and how sin separates between man and God. The ritual involved with the cleansing of the priests only served to show individual Israelites how easily they could be defiled. One cause of defilement was death, and therefore the law included detailed instructions about handling dead bodies. How then could God be sanctified when the bodies of Nadab and Abihu were desecrating the tabernacle? They needed removing from both the sanctuary and the camp. Aaron could not do this, for he was high priest and all in his office were strictly forbidden to have any contact with the dead (Leviticus 21:10-12). Though priests that were not on duty could attend to the bodies of near family members (verses

* See *Undesigned Scriptural Coincidences*, J J Blunt, pages 64-66. The prohibition carries over into the New Testament, for bishops or overseers were to be men "not given to wine" (1 Timothy 3:3).

86

2,3), Aaron's other two sons were on duty, so they were also barred from undertaking the task.

The job fell to Aaron's cousins, sons of his uncle, who carried the corpses away from the camp,* still in their priestly robes. Though the special clothing – especially for the high priest – was "for glory and for beauty" (Exodus 28:2), it could only represent what the priests were intended to be. The robes could not provide any supernatural protection for the men who wore them. By being disobedient to God, Nadab and Abihu desecrated both the office of priesthood, and thus the robes that were symbolic of that office.

Setting the Example

As the bodies were removed, Aaron and his two remaining sons were instructed to refrain completely from mourning, and to stay within the confines of the tabernacle, "lest ye die: for the anointing oil of the LORD is upon you" (Leviticus 10:7). As priests, they were to set the example for the nation, and despite their natural grief at the sudden death of their kinsmen, they were to show how obedience to God's word is of prime importance, even in circumstances involving emotional family ties.

The function of the priesthood needed clarifying urgently, lest this disaster recur again in the future, so God spoke specifically to Aaron. On all other occasions, Moses was charged with transmitting God's message, but this one was given directly to the high priest, instructing the priesthood to refrain from intoxicating liquor when on duty. The priests needed clear heads to undertake their important work on behalf of the people, to "put difference between holy and unholy, and between unclean and clean; and that ye may teach the children of Israel all the statutes which the LORD hath spoken" (verses 10,11). The prophet Malachi mentioned this twofold work when he spoke about the priesthood in his day, which was corrupt and ungodly: "he walked with me in peace and equity, and did turn many away from iniquity. For the priest's lips

---

* Blunt (pages 66-69) suggests that Mishael and Elzaphan, who removed the bodies, were those who could not keep the Passover in the second year because they were defiled by contact with a dead body (Numbers 9:6,7).

should keep knowledge, and they should seek the law at his mouth: for he is the messenger of the LORD of hosts" (Malachi 2:6,7).

The ceremony of consecration, which had been so rudely interrupted by Nadab and Abihu's presumption, had still to be completed. Moses instructed Aaron and his two remaining sons to continue with the priestly meal of portions from the various offerings, and he was horrified to discover that the priests' portion of the goat, which was offered for the sins of the people (see Leviticus 9:3), had been burnt. It was no longer available for them to eat. This effectively destroyed all the benefit that was to come to the people from having priests to minister on their behalf. The people's sin offering was "most holy, and God hath given it you (i.e., to the priests) to bear the iniquity of the congregation, to make atonement for them before the LORD" (10:17). Without the priests' involvement in the sacrifice, it would have no efficacy for the nation.

On the surface, at least, this error was just as serious as the one committed by Nadab and Abihu; God's commands were not followed. Moses reproached Eleazar and Ithamar, Aaron's remaining sons, who must have wondered if they would survive God's wrath, or perish like their older brothers. Aaron intervened and took full responsibility. He pleaded the recent shocking loss of his two oldest sons – "such things have befallen me" – and his belief that their death could have serious repercussions for him: "if I had eaten the sin offering today, would it have been well-pleasing in the sight of the LORD?" (verse 19, RV). How different is this attitude from the one shown by Aaron after he was involved in making the golden calf? On that occasion, he tried to shift the blame onto the people; this time he mediated on behalf of his sons, taking full responsibility, and the explanation was accepted.

A Faithful Priest

"Moses ... was content" (verse 20), and so, presumably, was God Himself. Because of the infirmity of the priesthood, so evident even at this earliest stage, there was a desperate need for an incorruptible priesthood. The need was identified, but Aaron's family did not supply it. Time and again through Israel's history there were priests whose weaknesses led them into corrupt and evil ways. A later prophet recorded God's judgement on Israel's priests: "They feed on the sin of my people; they are greedy for their iniquity. And it shall be like people, like priest; I will punish them for their ways, and requite them for their deeds" (Hosea 4:8,9, RSV). It was therefore revealed to Eli when his two sons also died before the Lord for their presumption: "I will raise me up a faithful priest, that shall do according to that which is in mine heart and in my mind: and I will build him a sure house" (1 Samuel 2:35).

By a supreme paradox, the failure of Nadab and Abihu, of Hophni and Phinehas and others, reinforced the fact that God would ultimately provide His faithful priest – a Son who would not fail, who would listen to God's commands and be obedient, and through whose death would be provided a way of cleansing and forgiveness.

SUMMARY OF NADAB AND ABIHU'S SIN

- at the end of the week of inauguration, Aaron's elder sons Nadab and Abihu offended by offering "strange fire" that was not acceptable to God
- through envy or pride they usurped their father Aaron's position, possibly also through intoxication which dulled their ability to discriminate
- the fiery glory which consumed the priestly sacrifices smote and killed Nadab and Abihu, confirming that God's commands must be followed diligently
- as the remaining priests would be defiled through contact with death, two of Aaron's cousins were commanded to remove the bodies
- Aaron and his two other sons were not to mourn while they were serving as priests
- as the priestly inauguration ceremony drew to a close it was discovered that a portion of one of the offerings, intended for priestly food, had unintentionally been burnt on the altar
- Aaron interceded successfully on behalf of his remaining two sons – he had learned an important lesson: his priesthood was "compassed with infirmity"

13

CLEAN AND UNCLEAN MEATS
Leviticus 11

IF the law's insistence on animal sacrifices seems strange to the modern disciple, even stranger are the requirements set out in the next section of Leviticus. Chapters 11–15 include details of dietary laws, childbirth, leprosy and bodily discharges, showing how easily a man or woman in Israel could be defiled, and stand in need of cleansing. Because these requirements do not apply to disciples of Christ, it is easy to conclude – as with animal sacrifices – that they hold no message or importance for today. Why then have these chapters been preserved? And why did the Lord Jesus direct his disciples to Leviticus when he told his disciples that they must be "perfect, even as your Father in heaven is perfect" (Matthew 5:48, cp. Leviticus 11:44)? We need to discover the answers to these questions before considering the chapters in detail.

In the analysis of Leviticus given in Chapter 4, chapters 11–15 were called "the Law of Purification". The chapters relate to discrimination in the things of everyday life, filling out God's command to the priests, "that ye may put difference between holy and unholy, and between unclean and clean" (Leviticus 10:10). The priests had a responsibility to instruct the people, and therefore the section commences with God uniquely speaking "unto Moses and to Aaron, saying unto them, speak unto the children of Israel …" (11:1,2).

Reasons for the Dietary Laws

This "law of purification" is in two parts: details of animals that were acceptable as food and those that were not (chapter 11); and various bodily matters relating to men and women in Israel (chapters 12–15). Chapter 11 forms an introduction to the section we are considering, and it is important to discover exactly what it teaches. Many commentators have been perplexed by the details of so-called 'clean' and 'unclean' animals, wondering what made one animal clean and another unclean, and various suggestions have been made over the years. The main alternatives are set out briefly as follows:

- *Idolatry:* God found the idolatrous worship of the Canaanites abominable, and the problem of "meats offered to idols" still existed as an issue of concern to the first century ecclesias. He therefore instructed His people to refrain from eating those animals that were used for sacrifice by the nations living in the land of promise.

- *National Separation:* By means of these dietary restrictions, Israelites would keep themselves separate from the surrounding nations. In support of the suggestion, it is often pointed out that Jews today with their strict kosher laws and regulations controlling the preparation of meat and dairy products remain a distinct and separate people.

- *Hygiene:* The restricted animals are often the ones that can carry disease. Pigs, for example, can transmit parasitic organisms, and it is suggested that the main reason for dietary laws was to fulfil God's promise to Israel: "I will put none of these diseases upon thee, which I have brought upon the Egyptians" (Exodus 15:26).

- *Allegorical Instruction:* A final suggestion is that the leading characteristics of the different animals would instruct the Israelites about the characteristics in mankind that are acceptable or unacceptable in God's sight: cloven feet indicate sure footedness; chewing the cud could explain the need to ruminate on spiritual food, etc.

When the Lord Jesus discussed with the people of his day the subject of bodily cleanliness and acceptable foods, he declared: "there is nothing from without a man, that entering into him can defile him" (Mark 7:15). The Gospel writer's comment on this was that Jesus thereby "declared all foods clean" (verse 19, RSV). There was, therefore, nothing intrinsically defiling in any food available to mankind. Yet Israel, as God's chosen nation, was commanded to distinguish between the different foods

God had provided for man's nourishment. This was symbolic of their special position in relation to Him: "I am the LORD your God, which have separated you from other people. Ye shall therefore put difference between clean beasts and unclean … and ye shall be holy unto me: for I the LORD am holy, and have severed you from other people, that ye should be mine" (Leviticus 20:24-26).

Sinful Man needs Cleansing

This key to understanding the emphasis on clean and unclean meats – that it is primarily to do with differences between people and not with any real or perceived differences between animals – is repeated in the New Testament when Peter receives instruction from God about the acceptability of Gentile converts. The vision he saw of a great sheet containing animals that the law of Moses defined as both clean and unclean was understood by Peter to teach him not to "call any *man* [whom God had cleansed] common or unclean" (Acts 10:28). The primary teaching of the dietary laws was thus not about animals, but about man himself: that he could be clean or unclean in God's sight; and if unclean, he stood in need of God's cleansing. Further support for this can be found in the sacrificial law, for those animals also represented the people who offered them. Once again, the emphasis was not on the animals, but upon the men and women who brought them, and upon their need for reconciliation. Animals do not need reconciling to God!

That mankind needs cleansing from sin is clearly the main teaching of the dietary laws, and it remains true today, therefore answering one of our opening questions about why the passages have been preserved for our instruction as well as for Israel of old. We must not, however, dismiss the other suggestions, for there were clearly secondary reasons for the law being enacted in this form for the people of Israel. By keeping close to its requirements, Israel was indeed kept distinct and different from the surrounding nations, and remarkably free from the diseases that plagued ancient peoples who had no understanding of simple hygienic measures. Furthermore, because the animals were representing different classes of mankind, there is also merit in the suggestion that the details may be allegorical, showing the qualities that are acceptable and unacceptable to God.*

Sin Separates Man from God

But primarily, as we have seen, men and women in Israel were taught on a daily basis as they selected food for their meals that they could easily be defiled, and thus become abominable in God's sight. They were being taught always to "refuse the evil, and choose the good" (cp. Isaiah 7:15,16). Essentially, the dietary law taught Israel about sin – which separates man from God – and about sinful man's need for atonement.

This message is confirmed in the chapters following the one about clean and unclean meats. Chapter 12 looks at childbirth, reminding the Israelites that once "sin entered into the world, and death by sin; so death passed upon all men, for that all have sinned" (Romans 5:12). Each newborn baby is conceived in, and enters into an environment of sin, with death as the certain end of its existence. Chapters 13 and 14 about leprosy emphasise the vileness and disfiguring nature of sin, showing that sin is indeed "exceeding sinful" (Romans 7:13), like a contagious disease. And chapter 15 with its message about bodily discharges graphically shows that sin is not external to man; as the Lord Jesus said: "evil things come from within, and defile the man" (Matthew 7:23).

A passage in the book of James confirms man's real problem. After listing the different categories of animals in the same order as in the dietary laws – beasts, birds, creeping things, and things in the sea – James says that "every kind (Greek, *phusis*, nature) of [animal] ... is tamed, and hath been tamed by mankind". He goes on to explain that, by comparison, no man can control his tongue: "it is an unruly evil, full of deadly poison" (James 3:7,8). Man is defiled by what he produces within himself, and not by what he takes in from without.

The overall theme of Leviticus 11–15, therefore, is man's inherent sinfulness, and how he needs to put

---

* A word of caution must be entered at this point. Without specific scriptural guidance, it is difficult to be certain that a particular allegorical interpretation is divinely intended.

himself right with God who is utterly holy. The information in these chapters confirms that holiness must be an everyday pursuit; it is not limited to occasions of formal worship, or when priests are present to minister on a person's behalf. The pursuit of holiness affects every part of a believer's life – his thoughts, his speech, his actions. This could not be expressed more forcefully than by impressing on the people of Israel the need to think about God's holiness every time they partook of food. The intention was clearly to make each Israelite ensure that his or her life conformed more closely to the character God wishes to see. The selection of food was therefore a means to an end, and certainly not the end itself.

Domestic Animals were 'Clean'

Chapter 11 establishes the general principles of the Jewish dietary laws, as they related to land animals (verses 2-8), sea creatures (verses 9-12), birds (verses 13-19), and insects (verses 20-23). The determining factor in each category seems to be that any departure from 'normal behaviour' was regarded as unclean. 'Normal' land animals – those with cloven hoofs that chew the cud – are generally those we would call domestic animals, i.e., those associated with man in his home life. As these were also the animals brought by the Israelites for their religious sacrifices, it is clear that they are intended to represent man in a state that is acceptable to God. Any behaviour that differs from this 'normal' state is unclean, defiling, and unacceptable to God — it cannot be offered acceptably to Him.

For the same reason there were certain physical blemishes that prevented priests from representing the Israelites in the presence of God. They were not to defile their appearance or have any external blemish; they were to conform to the 'normal' state of mankind (21:5,6,17-23). The prohibition appears harsh, until it is appreciated that the priests were symbolically representative of the people. The law regarding them was not condemning any individual; their physical features were used merely as symbols of moral behaviour.

What was true for land animals and the priesthood was also true for the other categories of the animal creation.

'Normal' sea creatures have fins and scales, and they were considered to be clean; all others were unclean. Turning to creatures that fly, the normal behaviour has to be deduced, for the law only lists unclean birds. These are generally birds of prey. Because they take life, which was an activity strictly forbidden for mankind, birds of prey were regarded as unclean. Insects that fly were also unclean. By flying, they were acting as birds, which is abnormal behaviour for "creeping things".

Through these details about different animals, the children of Israel were being taught that there is a way of life in mankind that God will accept – the way God intended him to live when he was created. Any deviation from that intention, forsaking God's instructions and commands, is sinful. God regards sin as a barrier between Himself and sinful man. Sin occurs when a man falls from God's likeness, and is defiled; he can only be cleansed by following the remedy God provided.

Defiled by Contact with Death

Not only were the unclean species to be considered unsuitable for food, their dead bodies were to be viewed as contaminating anyone who touched them: "whosoever toucheth the carcase of them shall be unclean until the even. And whosoever beareth ought of the carcase of them shall wash his clothes, and be unclean until the even" (verses 24,25). In line with the conclusion already reached, that 'unclean animals' represent sinful human behaviour, their carcases showed the certain end of all who fail to uphold God's righteousness – both sin and death erect a barrier between man and the living God who is of purer eyes than to behold evil.

Even 'clean' animals could only be eaten if they were specifically killed for food, and brought before God as an offering (17:2-4). If a clean animal died naturally its carcase was the same as the carcase of an unclean animal: "he that toucheth the carcase thereof shall be unclean until the even" (11:39). Every dead animal therefore reminded man of God's declaration in Eden. Because of sin, God said to Adam, "thou shalt surely die" (Genesis 2:17).

95

Because death is the natural and just consequence of sin, it is viewed in the law with the same abhorrence as the act of sin itself. Contact with a dead carcase made a person unclean, because death affects mankind only because of the existence of sin. To touch or carry a dead body, or part of one, made a person ritually unclean, as we have seen. This is further emphasised if the carcase of a dead animal should come in contact with a household item: it too was made unclean (Leviticus 11:32-35). We should note that it is "household" items that are involved. This is a similar point to the "cleanness" of domestic animals: both point unmistakably to individual men and women in Israel, who were susceptible to defilement because of the prevalence of sin and death. They too were "household objects" and could become unclean. Some of these items, "of wood, or raiment, or skin, or sack" were cleansed by immersion in water (verse 32). But earthen vessels contaminated by contact with a dead body could not be cleansed: "ye shall break it" (verse 33).

As all these items represent different classes of mankind, Israel was being taught about the stark realities of sinfulness. Unless a man submits to the cleansing power of God's word of salvation by being faithfully baptized in water, he will ultimately be broken, like the earthen vessel he is by nature. It was a call to personal holiness, and thereby to fellowship with God. If the Israelites remembered to cleave to that which was good, and refuse to be defiled by evil, then God would act on their behalf. His holiness was to encourage holiness in His people: "For I am the LORD that bringeth you up out of the land of Egypt, to be your God: ye shall therefore be holy, because I am holy" (verse 45).

SUMMARY OF THE DIETARY LAWS

- Laws about clean and unclean animals were not really about potential defilement from food, but about moral defilement from sin
- Every time an Israelite ate his food, he was reminded how easily he could be defiled by sin
- The dietary laws taught Israel that sin separates between man and God; holiness draws man nearer to God
- Clean animals conformed to 'normal' behaviour, and represented man in his created state – conforming to God's image
- Unclean animals did not conform in type or behaviour – they represented man when he strays from God's purpose and transgresses
- The carcases of clean and unclean animals defiled anything they touched, showing that death is the natural consequence of sin
- Vessels contaminated by death reminded Israelites of their own position before God – like those vessels they had either to be cleansed or destroyed

14

THINGS FROM WITHIN DEFILE THE MAN
Leviticus 12,15

ACCORDING to Israel's dietary laws all animal life was classified as either clean and acceptable for food, or unclean and therefore to be avoided. By an ancient application of the modern dietician's dogma – "you are what you eat" – anyone eating an unclean animal was reckoned to be unclean and in need of cleansing. Yet, as we have seen, these laws must be understood on the basis of the apostle's comment, "first ... that which is natural; and afterward that which is spiritual" (1 Corinthians 15:46). They were not about what went into the body, but about what came out. Men and women in Israel were being taught that whereas the behaviour of animals is fixed – no unclean animal could possibly make itself clean, and no clean animal could make itself unclean – human beings have free will: they can choose to honour God and obey Him, or they can choose to reject Him. Clean animals therefore represented men and women who were faithful to God's word and who sought to practise holiness; unclean animals represented those who were defiled by their sins.

Yet the question must still be asked, Why did God command these laws, if there were no animals that were intrinsically defiling? The answer is that man was being put to the test for his own ultimate good, and for his eternal well being. The test was godliness, and the aim was holiness or true communion between man and God. As Jesus explained, "he that is faithful in that which is least is faithful also in much: and he that is unjust in the least is unjust also in much" (Luke 16:10). The Israelite who rejected God's commands about the food he should eat could just as easily reject His teaching about the sanctity of life or marriage, and about the need for truth and integrity at all times. There could be no excuse, "For whosoever shall keep the whole law, and yet offend in one point, he is guilty of all" (James 2:10).

Uncleanness from Within

In the details of the law, men and women in Israel were encouraged to look carefully at themselves and appreciate that man is "of the earth, earthy", yet he is called to heavenly things. Not only could the food that he ate be unclean, even natural bodily functions were a perpetual reminder that man falls short of God's holiness: "Thou shalt have a place also without the camp ... and it shall be, when thou wilt ease thyself abroad, thou ... shalt turn back and cover that which cometh from thee: for the LORD thy God walketh in the midst of thy camp ... therefore shall thy camp be holy: that he see no unclean thing in thee" (Deuteronomy 23:12-14). The problem lay in what issued from within each individual, forcefully teaching where man's real problem lay – deep within himself. The potential for defilement was therefore ever present, and this was revealed particularly in matters of reproduction and childbirth, the subjects of Leviticus chapters 12 and 15.

Defilement was serious, because its effect was to put a person out of covenant relationship with God: the man or woman who was defiled was, at least temporarily, out of fellowship and in need of cleansing.

Leviticus 15 concerns discharges that come from within men and women: both those that occur naturally, and those that occur through abnormal circumstances. But only discharges from the sexual and reproductive organs are mentioned, even though there can be loathsome and physically defiling eruptions from other parts of the body. The purpose of the law was therefore to reveal an underlying moral and spiritual message, and the physical aspects were simply the medium by which the spiritual lessons were explained. The dietary law introduced the subject of defilement and man's need for cleansing from sin and its effects. The next stage in the message reveals that in mankind the propensity to sin is hereditary, and reaches back to our first parents who were presented with the aim of holiness but chose instead the path of rebellion. This message is reinforced in Leviticus 12 by the details of purification following childbirth, and in chapter 15 by the concentration on discharges from the reproductive organs. Each new generation simply confirmed that sinfulness is endemic in the human race.

Emphasis on Reproduction

There is merit in looking at some of the details in Leviticus 15 before considering the chapter on childbirth. By including separate details of male and female discharges it is clear that there is an emphasis on gender and sex – the message is not about boils or ulcers, or bodily discharges generally. The information is highly specific. The chapter can be divided into four parts:

- Abnormal male sexual discharges: i.e., gonorrhoeal* (verses 1-15)
- Normal male sexual discharges: i.e., seminal (verses 16-18)
- Normal female sexual discharges: i.e., menstrual (verses 19-24)
- Abnormal female sexual disharges: i.e., uterine haemorrhaging (verses 25-30)

The normal discharges led under the law to specified periods of uncleanness: "until the even" in the case of a man, and for "seven days" in the case of a woman. The different periods of separation are related to the extent of the discharges, which last longer in women than in men. Individuals emitting the discharge could not engage in worship or service until the stated period of separation was concluded and they had washed themselves completely with water. Each individual man or woman in Israel was expected to comply with the provisions of the law. Because these were natural discharges, they did not have to present themselves before the priest or offer a burnt offering or a sin offering. The message of the law was clear, however, there was the potential for defilement, and precautionary measures needed taking. The law taught that defilement is contagious, so physical contact with the discharge by other individuals also rendered them unclean "until the even",

---

* "Issue" (Hebrew *zowb*), in Leviticus 15:3, etc., is translated in the Septuagint by the Greek, *gonorrhues*.

when they too had to wash themselves completely with water (verses 18,19). In the woman's case, even natural discharges had further potential for defilement. In addition to direct contact, there was the possibility of indirect transmission of the uncleanness: for example, "whosoever toucheth her bed shall ... be unclean" (verses 21-23). This can be illustrated as follows:

Person with natural sexual discharge	Defiles by direct contact	Defiles by indirect contact
Man with a discharge	1. himself	–
	2. another person	–
	3. any object	–
Woman with a discharge	1. herself	–
	2. another person	–
	3. any object	Person who touches the object

Childbirth

This "indirect defilement" helps to explain an apparent difficulty in the chapter about childbirth. When a woman gave birth to a baby boy, she was considered to be unclean. Childbirth obviously bore a relationship to a woman's menstrual cycle, and part of her uncleanness was for "seven days; as in the days of her customary impurity" (Leviticus 12:2, NKJV).* After her son was circumcised and became a member of God's covenant nation, she continued in her separation for a further thirty-three days, making forty days in all. This period of separation ended when the woman brought a sin offering to the priest, to "make an atonement for her; and she shall be cleansed from the issue of her blood" (verse 7).

If, however, she bore a baby girl, the period of her separation for uncleanness was doubled: fourteen days "as

---

* This first period of separation, being similar to the one during a woman's menstrual flow, involved both the woman and anyone or anything she touched becoming unclean. The second period, after the child was circumcised, only affected the woman herself.

in her customary impurity", and another sixty-six days, making eighty days in all. It was like a secondary or indirect defilement, and we need to enquire why this was appropriate in the case of girl babies and not boy babies, just as it was with a woman's menstrual discharge, but not with a man's seminal discharge.

Each aspect of the law relating to defilement in chapters 12 and 15 emphasises the hereditary nature of man's susceptibility to sin. It was impossible for conception to occur without the man and the woman being temporarily unclean (15:18),* plainly declaring that human life is marred by sin right from its source. David acknowledged this in the Psalm he wrote after his sin with Bathsheba: "Behold, I was shapen in iniquity; and in sin did my mother conceive me" (Psalm 51:5). It was also confirmed by the uncleanness experienced by the woman as a result of childbirth. Every newborn child is a potential sinner, or as the Apostle Paul described it, "by one man's disobedience many were made sinners" (Romans 5:19). This prophecy was fulfilled again each time a child was born, and was acknowledged by the mother bringing a sin offering at the conclusion of her period of separation. When the child was a girl, not only was a potential sinner born, but a potential future mother was brought into the world, with the promise of yet another sinful generation to come. This was indicated by the period of separation being doubled when a girl was born, forcefully teaching that the human race perpetuates the sin of its first parents. The secondary defilement arising from a woman's menstrual discharge taught the same lesson: each new generation is a generation of sinners.

Unclean Practices

Returning to Leviticus 15, the details of normal sexual discharges leads to regulations about abnormal discharges in men and in women. Such complaints would often arise through unclean sexual practices, associating

* As sexual intercourse caused temporary uncleanness "until the even" for the man and the woman, the children of Israel were implicitly forbidden from adopting the Canaanite practice of shrine prostitutes when they worshipped at the tabernacle or Temple.

physical uncleanness even more closely to moral impurity. The much more serious nature of these situations is immediately apparent from the actions required of the individuals who suffered the discharges, and from the contagion of the illness (see table below). Whereas with normal discharges, the response showed there was potential for defilement, and the hygienic measures were mainly precautionary, with abnormal discharges the individual was actually unclean. The cleansing process commenced only *after* the discharge had ceased to flow.

When a person suffered an abnormal discharge, more attention had to be paid to cleansing. It was not sufficient to bathe completely, but the bathing had to be in "running" or "living" water (15:13), speaking of life and cleansing; and offerings had to be brought to the priest – two doves or pigeons, one as a burnt offering, the other as a sin offering. Although the sacrifices are mentioned in this order, they would actually be offered in the reverse order, for as we have already noted, a sin offering was always offered first. The burnt offering is mentioned first on this occasion because the most serious consequence of uncleanness is the breach in fellowship with God. Men and women showed their desire to be restored to fellowship by bringing a burnt offering, and its implicit promise of rededication.

The Law relating to Human Sexual Discharges				
Source & nature of sexual discharge	Period of separation	Action for cleansing	Offerings & sacrifice	Defilement by contact
Male – normal	Until even	Wash completely	None	Direct only
Female – normal	7 days	Wash completely	None	Direct & indirect
Male – abnormal	7 days from cessation of discharge	Bathe in running water	Sin offering & burnt offering	Direct & indirect
Female – abnormal	7 days from cessation of discharge	?	Sin offering & burnt offering	Direct & indirect

Woman with an Issue of Blood

The New Testament refers to these provisions when a woman "diseased with an issue of blood twelve years" approached Jesus for healing (Matthew 9:20-22). According to the law, anyone she touched was defiled, and any object coming in contact with her was made unclean and became a source of secondary defilement. Her illness kept her for twelve years from any intimate relationship, and from all communal worship. She could not be restored to normal life so long as the discharge continued, and therefore she sought help from doctors who were powerless to assist.

The marvel of this case lies in the woman's understanding. Her action expressed her acceptance of the Apostle's words: "What the law could not do in that it was weak through the flesh, God did by sending his own Son in the likeness of sinful flesh, on account of sin" (Romans 8:3, NKJV). She wanted to be restored, and knew that cleansing could come only through God's appointed priest. Salvation came to her, not through the law, but by her faith in Jesus Christ.

She knew of the contagion of uncleanness, and realised the truth of the statement, "Bad company ruins good morals" (1 Corinthians 15:33, RSV). The only antidote was to get herself in good company, and in the presence of one with godly morals. She understood how God would reverse the process of defilement, by intervening in human affairs through the gift of His Son. Where every other child born into this sinful world followed the example of Adam and sinned, Jesus was the only exception. Women, even if they were never unclean like her, suffered ritual defilement every month, and each time they gave birth. There was a constant reminder of sin, generation after generation. Each new child came from sinful stock, and produced sinful offspring. They, as well as she, were saved by the birth of God's child (cp. 1 Timothy 2:15), by whom mankind's unerring descent to the grave was halted, and through whom men and women are invited into fellowship with the Father.

The provisions in the law about discharges had a simple, but vitally important objective: "Thus shall ye separate the children of Israel from their uncleanness; that they die not in their uncleanness, when they defile my tabernacle that is among them" (Leviticus 15:31).

The final section of the Law of Purification, concerning the disease of leprosy, showed Israel how God views sin and its effects. This is the subject of the next chapter, but we should note that it occurs in Leviticus sandwiched between the instructions concerning sexual discharges and childbirth.

SUMMARY OF LAWS ABOUT DISCHARGES AND CHILDBIRTH

- Man is defiled by what comes out of him more than by what goes into him
- Reproduction and childbirth are mentioned in the Law of Purification to emphasise that the potential to sin is hereditary
- Childbirth was also ritually defiling because each new generation will commit sin
- All sexual discharges made a person unclean, as well as whoever he or she touched
- In the case of women, their uncleanness could be spread indirectly through any inanimate objects they touched
- A mother was unclean twice as long after giving birth to a girl, than if she bore a boy, because baby girls are potential mothers who can give birth to another sinful generation
- Cleansing of abnormal defilement could only be achieved by washing in running water, and by bringing offerings to God
- An individual who was cleansed was welcomed back into the fellowship of God's covenant people

---

15

LEPROSY AND SIN
Leviticus 13,14

THROUGH their national dietary laws Israelites were taught to distinguish between different foods with the intention that they would learn to distinguish between behaviour that is defiling, and a way of life that pursues holiness. Yet generation after generation produced nothing but more and more sinners, a fact that was starkly underlined by the ritual defilement attaching to conception and childbirth in Israel. Ever since the days of Adam, sin was in the world, "and death by sin" (Romans 5:12). Through the effects of this mortality, man is bodily weak and susceptible to illness; and morally he is predisposed to temptation and sin. The connections between sinfulness, illness and death are so strong that the law taught Israel about sin and its effects by focusing on a particularly loathsome form of disease called leprosy.

There has been much discussion about the exact nature of biblical leprosy (called in Hebrew *sara'at*, from a root word meaning 'to strike'), and many commentators doubt that modern leprosy is intended, but merely a serious skin complaint akin to psoriasis.* The Greek Septuagint translation of the Hebrew word *sara'at* is *lepra*, and this was carried over into the Latin Vulgate version, leading translators generally to use the term 'leprosy' in English language versions of the Bible. The Jewish Tanakh, however, translates the word as "a scaly affection on the skin"; and the NIV as "an infectious (or malignant, NEB) skin disease". In the absence of any specific information, and because even medical experts cannot agree, it may be

---

* It is difficult to see, however, how psoriasis could lead to Aaron's shocked reaction when Miriam was smitten by leprosy: "Let her not be as one dead, of whom the flesh is half consumed when he cometh out of his mother's womb" (Numbers 12:12).

wiser to consider the information available to us in the scriptures, and simply note the details of the disease and how they relate to human sinfulness. For this, and not any modern medical diagnosis, is the main objective of the legislation given to Israel.

Identifying Features

A further indication that we are not intended to discover any specific modern disease is that the same description (*sara'at*) is used about "diseases" like mildew and mould in clothing and buildings. Once again, it is the connection between particular aspects of these complaints and human sinfulness that is important, and not the identification of the physical problems themselves. Bringing these details together paints a very graphic picture, not only of the disease, but of the fundamental problem of sin:

- The disease starts from very small beginnings, which can be detected once they are more than skin deep.
- Once the disease takes hold, it is likely to spread quickly, revealing "raw flesh".
- The disease eventually affects the whole person, and easily passes to others who become affected by it.
- The person who has the disease must therefore be treated as an outcast, or as a mourner at his or her own funeral.
- If the disease is found in clothing or fabric, it must be destroyed by burning if it spreads, or carefully washed if it does not spread.
- If the disease is discovered in a building, the affected stones must be removed completely and replaced; if the disease recurs, the whole building must be destroyed.

In every case, the identification is undertaken by the priest who has to look carefully for signs of the disease's presence and development, and whether there should be periods of temporary quarantine or outright banishment.

Why Leprosy?

Why is there so much concentration on leprosy and not on other diseases that can be equally distressing and possibly even more life-threatening? What about diseases of the blood or the respiratory system, or any of the other types of disease that plague mankind? We have noted, in the case of bodily discharges, that only those relating to the sexual organs are mentioned in Leviticus 15 in order to draw attention to the fact that sinfulness passes from generation to generation. Similarly, the law's concentration on leprosy, rather than on illness in general, draws attention dramatically to the nature of sin, to sin's effect on the sinner, and to its effect upon all who come in contact with his or her sin.

There is a further problem. All these factors could be shown by looking only at leprosy as it affects men and women. Why is there additional information about so-called 'leprosy' in clothing and in buildings? And, if 'leprosy' can affect clothes and buildings, what about other inanimate objects? Why are they not mentioned? Right from the earliest occurrence in scripture, clothing is related to the covering that is needed for sin: first the covering Adam and Eve hurriedly prepared from fig leaves, and then the covering God supplied, which was symbolic of the salvation He would provide through the work of His Son (Genesis 3:7,21). Christ's righteousness is the covering of those who identify with him through faith and baptism, and it is possible to defile this covering by failing to acknowledge the continuing dependence true disciples have in the Lord.

Garments Spotted by Flesh

Jesus commented that there were a few in the ecclesia in Sardis who had not defiled their garments (Revelation 3:4), and revealed a vision of others who had "washed their robes, and made them white in the blood of the Lamb" (7:14). Not to seek benefit from the forgiveness provided by Christ's sacrifice is to let the garment of salvation become "spotted by the flesh" (Jude 23). This last reference, with its echoes of Leviticus 13 ("garment", "flesh", "spotted"), clearly links the unrepented and unforgiven sins of disciples with the leprous garments that under the law had to be inspected every seven days, and either washed or destroyed by fire.

Similarly, leprosy in the fabric of a house pointed to problems in a house where there are disciples – what the

Apostle Paul calls "the house of God, which is the church of the living God" (1 Timothy 3:15). The law therefore teaches that sin can affect the ecclesia of God, and if it is left untreated it can spread throughout the house, ultimately reaching the stage where only one solution can be applied – total destruction.

The details in Leviticus 13 and 14 about leprosy have therefore been revealed and preserved to teach mankind about sin – individual offences, sins committed by anyone in covenant relationship with God, and sins that affect God's covenant people in their association with each other. These three aspects of sin are all related, and therefore they are all described by reference to the same disease: leprosy.

Individual Offences

The principal teaching is about personal sins. Whenever anyone in Israel noticed an unusual blemish on his skin, he had to present himself before the priest, whose visual inspection determined if the blemish was leprous. In every case, "the priest shall look" (Leviticus 13:3,5,6,8, etc.), and there were three possible conclusions he could reach. If signs of leprosy were clearly present, he declared the person to be unclean, and the leper was separated completely both from society and from communal worship. If the distinctive signs of leprosy were not present, but the skin was clearly blemished, the priest could not be sure if leprosy was in its early stages. He therefore put the person in quarantine for seven days to see what happened, and inspected him again a week later. All doubt would by then be removed, and the person was either declared leprous and unclean, or free from leprosy and clean.

Signs that leprosy was present included the following: when hairs in the affected area turned white or yellow; when the blemish appeared more than skin deep; and when raw flesh was visible. The natural feelings of repulsion that are experienced when Leviticus 13 is read were much greater when leprosy was actually present and visible, and there would be a deep sense of shame when the man or woman with the disease approached the priest dressed in his holy robes. This great contrast between the leper and the priest is clearly intentional. Israelites were being forcefully taught about the difference between their sinful state, and what God really wanted them to be. The priest and the Nazarite presented the qualities of holiness that God was seeking from every Israelite: they were separated to God and separated from sin. By contrast, the leper displayed every characteristic of sin, and he displayed it in such a way that his disease – like sin itself – was repulsive.

The details of leprosy in individuals start with general skin blemishes (Leviticus 13:2-17), then deal with blemishes arising on the site of previous injuries (verses 18-28), and conclude with blemishes on the skin of the head (verses 29-44). The significance of this is generally masked by all the details of the disease, but as soon as it is recognised that the real message of the chapter is about sin, it is apparent that sin can occur in any part of a person's life, and certainly where it has appeared before, because everyone has "besetting sins". Finally, by talking about a "plague in his head" (verse 44), the law acknowledges the truth of the Lord's comments about how sin always starts in the mind with evil thoughts.

This understanding of the passage is confirmed by the consequences for the leper when he was declared unclean (verses 45,46). He had to rend his clothes, bare his head and cover his lips, as if he was mourning (cp. 10:6; Ezekiel 24:17); he had to warn others of his condition by shouting, "Unclean, unclean", lest they come in contact with him and be defiled; and he was banished from the camp and normal society: "he shall dwell alone; without the camp shall his habitation be" (Leviticus 13:46). More than a mourner, he was like a living corpse. Although he was alive, he was treated as if he was dead, mourning his own demise.

Was it possible for the message to be declared more graphically that sin, unless it is forgiven, leads inevitably to unending death? With leprosy, the body first grew insensible, then began to decompose while the person was still alive, and the corrupting flesh taught unerringly about the corrosive effect of sin. The message about the leper was like a great parable of the human condition: bodily corruption is the expression and outcome of moral corruption. By putting the leper outside the camp, he was separated from all normal social contact. But more importantly still, he was separated from the opportunity to worship, and therefore from God Himself. So clearly and finally does sin separate a man or woman from God.

Leprosy in Clothing

When we turn to the information about diseased clothing, there is a further unusual aspect. Not only is it strange for clothing to be diseased, but in contrast to the disease of leprosy in human flesh, this disease hurts! For when a diseased garment was declared leprous, the priest announced that "the plague was a *fretting* leprosy", meaning a leprosy that is painful, or that irritates (verse 51).* Any garment with fretting leprosy had to be destroyed by burning. Clothes that had early signs of leprosy, but where the disease did not spread, could be salvaged either by washing, or by tearing out and burning the diseased section.

Again the message about sin is clear. Anyone who benefits from God's salvation in Christ, and then turns away to commit his life to the way of sin, crucifies the Son of God afresh, and puts him to an open shame (Hebrews 6:6). Sin is painful in one whose conscience has previously caused him to be baptized, and it has to be tackled urgently and decisively, lest the garment of righteousness be permanently defiled.

Leprosy in a House

Even more serious is the situation when leprosy is discovered in a house, and once again, when it exists it is painful – a fretting leprosy. The law was acknowledging the fact that believers, "as lively stones, are built up a spiritual house" (1 Peter 2:5), and that when sin exists in the ecclesia it can be painful and destructive.

The treatment for an affected house required first the removal of diseased stones and of all internal plaster to check if the leprosy had spread to other stones. New stones and new plaster replaced what was taken outside the city to an unclean place (Leviticus 14:40-42). If this did

---

* The word occurs outside Leviticus 13 & 14 only in Ezekiel 28:24, where it describes Israel's hostile neighbours as *"pricking* briers".

not eradicate the problem, it was deep-seated – a fretting leprosy requiring the total demolition and removal of the house.

A later reference to these provisions confirms that the message was more about Israel's spiritual house than about problems of mould or disease in literal buildings. Zechariah saw a vision of God's judgement on His faithless people, and said: "it shall enter into the house of the thief, and into the house of him that sweareth falsely by my name: and it shall remain in the midst of his house, and shall consume it with the timber thereof and the stones thereof" (Zechariah 5:4; cp. Leviticus 14:45).

Cleansing

None of the measures taken in response to leprosy were able to cure it; at best, they helped to contain its effects. If its progress ceased, and the skin no longer showed the identifying signs of the presence of leprosy, the priest was able to declare the leper clean, and special sacrifices had to be offered before the cleansed leper could re-enter society and join again in communal worship.

The first part of the sacrifice comprised two "clean" birds, cedar wood, scarlet and hyssop. One of the birds was killed in an earthen vessel over running water. The remaining bird, the cedar wood, the scarlet and the hyssop were dipped into the blood collected in the earthen vessel, and used to sprinkle the blood seven times over the cleansed leper before the living bird was released. The whole operation was full of significance. The leper had been as good as dead, and now was clean. The earthen vessel showed that death comes to all who are of the earth, earthy, and that life is a gift from God. The man had been as one dead, like the slain bird; now he was free, and like the living bird he was let "loose into the open field", free to come and go as he chose (Leviticus 14:7). The hyssop and scarlet spoke of purification and healing, and the cedar wood of freedom from corruption.

The ritual was not yet complete. Before he could enter the camp again, the cleansed leper had to wash and shave himself completely. On the completion of this act he was welcomed back into the camp, but not yet into his own tent. Seven days later he washed and shaved himself again before approaching the tabernacle with two male lambs, one ewe lamb and a quantity of oil. One lamb was offered as a trespass offering in acknowledgement of the period when the leper was unable to worship God; the second as a sin offering because of his uncleanness; and the last as a burnt offering to dedicate his future life to God's service. The blood of the trespass offering and the oil were smeared on the leper's right ear, right thumb, and the big toe of his right foot. Any remaining oil was poured over his head.

All this is very reminiscent of other ceremonies, and the connection is very significant. When Aaron and his sons were inaugurated as priests they were anointed in a similar way (Leviticus 8:23,24); and when the Levites were appointed to assist in the priestly service, they too had to wash and shave themselves (Numbers 8:7). The stark difference between the diseased leper and the priest who had previously declared him unclean no longer existed. The disease taught about the corrupting effect of sin, and now he was cleansed the leper understood about the need for holiness if an Israelite was to worship God acceptably. Did not God expect His people to be a "kingdom of priests, and an holy nation" (Exodus 19:6)?

The washing and shaving indicated the new life into which the cleansed leper entered. Though he was an adult, he acknowledged that he was like a newborn child fresh from the womb;* and though he brought animals with him to be sacrificed, the priest had to offer them on his behalf – like an adult assisting a helpless child. By bringing these sacrifices, the cleansed leper was once again able to be involved in communal worship. But there was a distinct two-stage process. First, the leper was brought back into the camp, and after a week as a 'newborn' Israelite he entered fully into the life of God's covenant people on the eighth day. It was physically impossible for the leper to be circumcised again, but the week's delay was equivalent to the period between natural

* When Naaman the Syrian was cleansed from leprosy, the record specifically notes that "his flesh came again like unto the flesh of a little child" (2 Kings 5:14).

childbirth and circumcision when the Israelite formally became a member of the nation.

Cleansed by His Blood

Anyone involved in this ritual of cleansing also could not fail to notice the crucial importance of blood. The living bird which symbolised the leper's new life, and the other associated commodities were all dipped in the blood of the slain bird, confirming once again the great principle that without the shedding of blood there can be no remission of sins (Hebrews 9:22). The regulations surrounding the cleansed leper looked forward to a priest who could not only identify the presence of sin, but do something about it. He would have this authority because he lived a sinless life, and offered it in accordance with God's command to redeem and cleanse repentant sinners. The law of leprosy therefore declared divine teaching about sin and salvation as two related processes – one natural, the other spiritual; one in Adam, the other in Christ:

In Adam-----> *Sin*-------------> *Disease*-------->*Death*

In Christ----> *Forgiveness*--> *Healing*-------> *Eternal life*

While the law of leprosy looked forward to Christ's work, it also revealed its own inadequacy. Priests in Aaron's line could only observe and record whether leprosy existed, how it developed, and when its progress had ceased; they could not effect any cure whatsoever. Because of the defiling nature of the disease, their approach had to be distant; they could look but not touch, for defilement was contagious.

With the coming of Jesus came also a completely different arrangement. When a leper asked to be healed, Jesus, acknowledging that he could act where the law was powerless, stretched out his hand and touched him. In the process, the leper was cleansed (Matthew 8:2,3). As with the disease, so with sin. In Jesus, sins can be completely removed – but only because he identified completely with those he came to save. He touches us and can cleanse our hearts and minds, only because he first was "touched with the feeling of our infirmities ... yet without sin" (Hebrews 4:15).

After all that Leviticus says about sin and uncleanness, chapter 16 – which we shall consider next – explains the most important day in the religious calendar. The tenth day of the seventh month was the Day of Atonement when the nation was united in receiving mercy, forgiveness and reconciliation.

SUMMARY OF LAWS ABOUT LEPROSY

- Of all the diseases that afflict mankind, leprosy was highlighted by the law because it most closely represents sin and its effects
- Leprosy was identified by the priests if the disease was more than skin deep, had turned the hair white or yellow, or was revealing raw flesh
- Clothing and buildings could also be leprous, teaching about how the garment of salvation and the ecclesia can be defiled by sin
- When the disease occurred in clothes and buildings it could become a "fretting leprosy" – a disease with painful consequences
- Lepers were banished from society, and could not engage in public worship; like living corpses they had no contact with healthy people, and they were estranged from God
- When the disease affected clothes or buildings, the affected parts had to be removed before the disease spread completely
- On the rare occasions when the disease's progress halted, the priest could declare the leper clean
- Two birds were involved in response to his cleansing: one was killed, and the other was let free after being dipped in the dead bird's blood. One bird respresented the leper when he was banished; the other represented his new-found freedom
- In acknowledgement of his cleansing, the leper washed and shaved completely, becoming like a newborn child; he also brought animals to be sacrificed
- After eight days back in the camp, he was welcomed back fully into the nation and became part of God's covenant people – the equivalent of circumcision
- Whereas the law could only observe the disease and limit its effects, Jesus is able to cleanse us from our sins in his own blood

---

16

THE DAY OF ATONEMENT
Leviticus 16

THE opening verse of Leviticus 16 explains that the chapter is not in strict chronological order. It reveals that "the LORD spake unto Moses *after* the death of the two sons of Aaron" (Leviticus 16:1). Yet the account of the death of Nadab and Abihu appears in chapter 10, and details of the laws of uncleanness intervene before God's message to Moses at this critical time is recorded in chapter 16. We need if possible to discover why the material in Leviticus is ordered in this way. The table below shows the main sections of the first half of Leviticus and the impact of Nadab and Abihu's sin.

The chapters that appear before the account of Nadab and Abihu's sin explain the law of offerings and the appointing of Aaron's family as priests. The orderly situation envisaged by these early chapters was rudely disrupted by Nadab and Abihu's arrogance and disobedience, so that God had to declare: "I will be sanctified in them that come nigh me, and before all the people I will be glorified" (10:3). Israel was therefore provided with information showing that the problem of uncleanness was an ever-present danger. If priests were

The Impact of the Failure of the Aaronic Priesthood	
Chapters 1–7	Sacrifices and Offerings
Chapters 8,9	Consecrating the Priesthood
Chapter 10	**Nadab and Abihu's Sin and Death**
Chapters 11–15	Law of Defilement and Cleansing
Chapter 16	**The Day of Atonement**

not immune from sinning, how could the people possibly expect to remain free from personal defilement?

Even the sacrifices and offerings, so carefully detailed for people and priests, did not fully resolve the problem created by sin and uncleanness. Some serious breaches of God's commands were not covered by any of the sacrifices, and additionally there would be many occasions when even the most conscientious Israelite would not realise that he or she was commiting moral or ceremonial offences. Was the nation therefore condemned for ever to be separated from God, who had stated His desire to set His tabernacle among them and walk in their midst?

Restrictions on the High Priest

This was the background to God's message to Moses after Nadab and Abihu's death. Moses was instructed to tell Aaron that, despite his being appointed as high priest, he was not free to enter before God's presence at will – "into the holy place within the vail before the mercy seat, which is upon the ark" (Leviticus 16:2)*. If he ever chose to present himself uninvited, his life would be forfeit just like his sons'. This is the effect of sin. Aaron represented a sinful nation, and his sons had shown how sin affected every individual in Israel. God who is of purer eyes than to behold evil could not righteously overlook His people's transgressions.

He had however established the means whereby He could be approached – "I will be sanctified in them that come nigh me" – so He explained to Moses the terms on which Aaron could enter the most holy place. Only on one day in the year, a day specified in advance by God, and requiring special preparations on Aaron's behalf, the high priest was welcomed into God's presence to "make an atonement for the holy sanctuary ... for the tabernacle of the congregation and for the altar ... for the priests, and for all the people of the congregation" (verse 33).

The leading feature of the Day of Atonement for Israel was therefore the evidence it provides to show the absolute inadequacy of the law to save sinners and

---

* This prohibition provides further evidence that Nadab and Abihu actually had the effrontery to enter the most holy place.

reconcile them to God. All the activity under the law happened outside the most holy place, and in process of time even the tabernacle was defiled by this activity. This was further emphasised by the sanctuary and altar needing atonement every year. The offerings under the law did not fully cleanse from sin, so even the altar needed periodic cleansing, "because of the uncleanness of the children of Israel, and because of their transgressions, even (RV) all their sins" (verse 16). If the individual sacrifices had been efficacious, there would be no need for the cleansing arrangements on the Day of Atonement. Its enactment is a serious indictment of the law itself, an indictment confirmed in the Letter to the Hebrews, where the apostle comments on the fact that the most holy place was out of bounds for all except for one day each year: "the Holy Spirit this signifying, that the way into the holiest of all was not yet made manifest, while as the first tabernacle was yet standing: which was a figure for the time then present, in which were offered gifts and sacrifices, that could not make him that did the service perfect, as pertaining to the conscience" (Hebrews 9:8,9).

The Importance of the Seventh Month

The day in the year set aside by God for the high priest to enter the most holy place was "the seventh month, on the tenth day of the month" (Leviticus 16:29). The seventh month was the busiest in the religious calendar, starting on the first day of the month with the "memorial of blowing of trumpets", and containing the most joyful of all the feasts, the feast of tabernacles, running from the fifteenth day for eight consecutive days. Under the law, the seventh month typified the great day of rest that "remaineth … to the people of God" (Hebrews 4:9), and it was fitting that a great atonement should precede the feast of tabernacles, where God's great bounty was remembered annually with deep thankfulness. The special features of the Day of Atonement gave a divine explanation of the true rest to which God was calling His people: "on that day shall the priest make an atonement for you, to cleanse you, that ye may be clean from all your sins before the LORD. It shall be a sabbath of rest unto you, and ye shall afflict your souls, by a statute for ever"

(Leviticus 16:30,31). On the Day of Atonement, therefore, all in Israel were to rest from their sins because God promised to cleanse them from all their sins.

However, the forgiveness of the nation's sins was not unconditional. Another feature of the Day of Atonement showed how true forgiveness can only be based on heartfelt confession and repentance. Unique amongst the major religious festivals in Israel, the Day of Atonement was a day "to afflict your souls, and do no work" (verse 29; 23:27); it was therefore a fast and not a feast. God looked for humility in His people, such as the Psalmist showed when he was in trouble: "I humbled (afflicted, RV) my soul with fasting ... I bowed down heavily, as one that mourneth for his mother" (Psalm 35:13,14). There can hardly be a greater expression of distress than mourning the death of a parent, and this is how our Heavenly Father expects us to feel about sins that separate us from Him as surely as death removes our loved ones from us.

"A day to afflict the soul"

Aaron was in exactly this position, for the details of the Day of Atonement were given to him through Moses immediately after the death of Nadab and Abihu. Fittingly, therefore, Aaron was chosen to undertake the leading part on the Day of Atonement. He had to enter the most holy place six months* after his sons were killed for attempting to do the same. He represented the whole nation, though not on this occasion in a priestly capacity. His sons' disobedience revealed the failure of the Aaronic priesthood, and Aaron like everyone else in Israel stood in need of atonement. He was a fitting representative, for the remembrance of his sons' disobedience and death would certainly cause him to "afflict his soul" and consider his own unworthiness. Meantime, the people were also to afflict their souls. This one day in the year, if at no other time, was a day when human pride and boasting were to be subdued before the holiness of Almighty God. If the people refused, they would be punished like Nadab and Abihu: "For whatsoever soul it be that shall not be

---

* Assuming that Leviticus was written during the first month of the second year of Israel's wilderness journey, cp Exodus 40:17 and Numbers 1:1.

afflicted in that same day, he shall be cut off from among his people" (Leviticus 23:29). Implicitly acknowledging the failure of the priesthood, Aaron divested himself of his high priestly robes, and clothed himself in different holy garments. These were simple, undecorated items of clothing made from linen – coat, breeches, belt and mitre: "for the fine linen is the righteousness of saints" (Revelation 19:8).

The limitations of the priesthood under the law were also revealed by Aaron having to make atonement offerings for himself and his family (Leviticus 16:6). In the meantime, all other priests were barred from the Tabernacle (verse 17). On their behalf Aaron sacrificed a bullock as a sin offering. Only then could he present the sin offering on behalf of the people. This consisted of two goats. He had previously cast lots to determine which would be killed and which would be kept alive. The blood of the goat that was sacrificed was treated in the same way as the blood of the priests' bullock – it was sprinkled seven times towards the mercy seat while the most holy place was filled with a cloud of incense taken from the incense altar. The blood was also used to make atonement for the holy place, the tabernacle and the altar. This action acknowledged that the law had been broken and that it was unable to save sinners in Israel. Sprinkling the blood on the mercy seat was an appeal to God's mercy, asking Him to remember His covenant with the people and to fulfil it by forgiving their sins.

For Azazel

Attention now focuses on the other goat. As with the sacrifices when a leper was cleansed, two animals were used in order to show both the means and the effect of the cleansing. The sacrifice of the first goat showed that "without shedding of blood there is no remission" of sins (Hebrews 9:22, RV), whereas letting the other goat go free expressed the consequence of the forgiveness of sins granted to all in Israel as a result of God's mercy on the Day of Atonement. The goats had been selected by casting lots, one "for the LORD", one "for Azazel" (Leviticus 16:8, RV). Down through the centuries much confusion has arisen over the meaning and purpose of the term "azazel".

The original Hebrew word is a compound of *az*, meaning goat, and *azel*, meaning to go away or disappear. William Tyndale originally coined the term "scapegoat" in his translation of the scriptures to express the idea of 'the goat that escaped' (i.e., escaped death), while the translators of the Revised Version suggested an alternative, speaking of two goats – one for the LORD, the other "for dismissal" (16:8, RV margin).

The idea behind the term is obvious. One goat was sacrificed, and the other was dismissed or sent away. Escaping death, it became a living sacrifice bearing away the sins of the people. Echoes of the ceremony on the Day of Atonement elsewhere in the Old Testament confirm what was meant. The Psalmist said: "As far as the east is from the west, so far hath he removed our transgressions from us" (Psalm 103:12). Isaiah said, "Thou hast cast all my sins behind thy back" (Isaiah 38:17); and, speaking of the work of the Lord Jesus Christ, he proclaimed: "All we like sheep have gone astray; we have turned every one to his own way; and the LORD hath laid on him the iniquity of us all" (53:6).

Corrupted Meanings

After Aaron laid his hands on the head of the second goat and confessed the nation's sins, the animal was led away from the camp into the wilderness, "and the goat shall bear upon him all their iniquities unto a land not inhabited" (Leviticus 16:22). On one occasion, tradition asserts, this goat found its way back from the wilderness and entered into Jerusalem bringing consternation and not reassurance to the people. In subsequent years a different method was adopted and the goat "for removal" was led to the edge of a gully, where it fell to its death. "Azazel" thereafter became a term used by Jews to mean an evil all-consuming spirit, and "Go to Azazel!" is the Jewish equivalent of Christendom's curse, "Go to Hell!", or "Go to the Devil!".

Noting the Jewish practice on the Day of Atonement, the New English Bible translators rendered *azazel* in Leviticus 16:8 as "for the Precipice" – perpetuating the idea that is now comprehended by the modern use of Tyndale's word "scapegoat", as referring to one who is

121

blamed or punished for the sins of others. This is a serious distortion of the original meaning, and of the role of the second goat. In one sense the two goats cannot be separated; both formed the sin offering for the people. In the death of one and the preservation of the other were prefigured the crucifixion and resurrection of the Lord Jesus. The second goat was not punished for the sins of the people, but symbolically bore away their sins. The popular view preserves the erroneous idea of substitution – suffering instead of another – whereas the truth of the matter is that the goats were representative: their sacrifice was on behalf of men and women in Israel. In fact, the benefit of this national atonement was so generous that it extended even to the "stranger that sojourneth among you" (verse 29).

The goat for dismissal was led into "a land not inhabited (a land of separation, AV margin)", where it was "let go … in the wilderness" (verse 22). As the embodiment of Israel's sins, the goat was taken away from the camp where the people dwelt to show how their sins were removed from them, but it was also taken away from the sanctuary where God dwelt, showing how their sins were removed from before His face. Graphically and visibly the symbolism taught Israel about forgiveness. God's mercy was extended through an acceptable sacrifice and resulted in the complete removal of "all their sins" (verse 16).

Resuming the Priestly Role

Only then could Aaron resume his role as High Priest. He bathed in water and put on his garments "for glory and for beauty" (verses 23,24; Exodus 28:40), before completing the offerings on behalf of the priesthood and the nation. The fat of the sin offerings, the burnt offerings, and the disposal of the carcases were all handled in accordance with the measures enacted under the general law of sacrifices, showing how dependent the nation was on this special and unique act of atonement.

Once the special atonement offering was complete, the festive offerings of the seventh month could commence (Numbers 29:7-11), for the month was essentially one of joy, thanksgiving and celebration. Every fiftieth year (i.e., on average, once in every person's lifetime) this celebration reached a zenith, and the jubilee trumpet sounded: "in the day of atonement shall ye make the trumpet sound throughout your land" (Leviticus 25:9); for, "Blessed are they whose iniquities are forgiven, and whose sins are covered. Blessed is the man to whom the Lord will not impute sin" (Romans 4:7,8, citing Psalm 32:1,2).

SUMMARY OF DAY OF ATONEMENT

- Occurred only once each year, on the tenth day of the seventh month
- The seventh month looked forward to the great day of rest, and the Day of Atonement showed that true rest cannot exist unless Sin is removed
- The details of the day were given immediately following the death of Nadab and Abihu
- It would have been unnecessary if the law ministered by priests was able fully to cleanse sins
- On the Day of Atonement all in Israel were cleansed of all their sins
- It was a day for fasting and mourning, because sin separates mankind from God
- It was the only day in the year that the high priest could enter the Most Holy Place
- He could enter only after acknowledging his own sinfulness, and after putting on clean linen robes that represented righteousness
- After making a sin offering for himself and his family, he took two goats as a sin offering for the people
- He cast lots: one goat was for the Lord, the other for *azazel*, meaning "dismissal"
- The first goat was slain, and its blood sprinkled seven times towards the Mercy Seat
- The second goat, for azazel, was sent away into the wilderness after the high priest laid hands on its head and confessed over it the nation's sins
- Once the sin offerings were made, and the nation's sins were borne away into the wilderness, there could be thankfulness, rejoicing and celebration
- Every fiftieth year, the Day of Atonement signalled the start of the year of Jubilee

17

SEPARATE FROM THE NATIONS
Leviticus 17,18

ALL that Moses revealed to Israel about God's holiness, and how He must be sanctified in those who approach Him exposed the nation's inherent sinfulness. Even the most diligent and scrupulous Israelites committed sins that separated them from God, necessitating God's intervention to make provision for forgiveness and reconciliation to be extended. Many aspects of daily life could be morally defiling, and the nation was instructed about this by details in the law showing how easily physical and ritual defilement could occur through contact with unclean food, illness or death. The underlying problem in every case was the ever present tendency to sinfulness, and God wished His people to keep themselves free from sin by drawing ever closer to Him.

Further reinforcement of this teaching comes from the next section in Leviticus, starting in chapter 17. This introduces various subjects that all have one common theme: the need to follow God's judgements and ordinances, and showing how these stood in stark contrast to the practices that were so common in the surrounding nations. In Chapter 4 we called this section the 'Law of Holiness' (page 22).

Bring Sacrifices to the Tabernacle

It commences by explaining the importance of animal sacrifices under the law. During Israel's wilderness wanderings, every animal that was killed had to be brought to the tabernacle and offered as a peace (or fellowship) offering to God.* No other practice was acceptable. Life is precious in God's sight; He both gives life and takes it away. Anyone who sheds blood has to

---

* For practical reasons, this legislation was repealed once Israel occupied the land of Canaan (Deuteronomy 12:20-25).

acknowledge that he has trespassed on divine territory, and needs to act in order to restore the relationship God seeks to have with His people. But the requirement to bring every animal to the tabernacle also had another important purpose; it was to prevent the continuation of what the Israelites were familiar with in Egypt, where sacrifices were made to many different deities: "to the end that the children of Israel may bring their sacrifices, which they* offer in the open field, even that they may bring them unto the LORD" (Leviticus 17:5). Punishment for disobedience was death ("that man shall be cut off from among his people", verses 4,9, etc.).

By describing the forbidden sacrifices as being made "in the open field", it is apparent that many of the deities worshipped in Egypt were so-called 'gods of nature', whom the Egyptians wished to appease in order to obtain blessings of storehouse and barn. Further to reinforce the message that the restriction was specifically to prevent idolatry, God emphatically stated: "they shall no more offer their sacrifices unto devils, after whom they have gone a whoring" (verse 7). The "devils" referred to here were satyrs (Hebrew, sa'ir, goat, hairy) like the later Greek god Pan, whose worship involved many obscene and lewd practices. The comment that Israel went "a whoring" after such gods was therefore literally as well as spiritually true.

Other aspects of this "devil" worship involved abuse of the blood of the sacrificed animals, causing God to declare that eating blood was unacceptable to Him. It obscured all that godly sacrifice taught Israel about the importance of blood in representing the life which God requires to be given wholly to Him: "Ye shall eat the blood of no manner of flesh: for the life of all flesh is in the blood thereof: whosoever eateth it shall be cut off" (verse 14).

Egypt and Canaan were Idolatrous

The slaughter and sacrifice of animals as part of idolatrous religion has a very ancient history, and Israel was beguiled and attracted because of the often sensual

---

* i.e. those of other nations, notably the Egyptians, whose ways were quickly copied by Israel.

nature of idol worship. These obscene practices were not
limited to animal sacrifices, however, but infiltrated many
aspects of daily life, as the 'Law of Holiness' goes on to
reveal. God had brought His people out of Egypt, and was
leading them to His land, where it was possible for the
nation to break with the past and make a fresh start.
However, it proved much easier physically to take Israel
out of Egypt, than to remove ungodly Egyptian thoughts
and ways from the Israelite people. To make matters worse,
the inhabitants of Canaan had similar ungodly practices,
making God declare to Israel: "After the doings of the land
of Egypt, wherein ye dwelt, shall ye not do: and after the
doings of the land of Canaan, whither I bring you, shall ye
not do: neither shall ye walk in their ordinances" (18:3). He
encouraged Israel to remain true to His teachings.

After showing that the law of sacrifice should not be
abused, the next measures targeted the gross immorality
that often accompanied idolatry by specifying sexual
relationships that were forbidden because of the close
blood relationship between the parties. As with other
aspects of the law, there were both practical and spiritual
reasons underlying these measures. The practical purpose
of these regulations involved the fact that offspring born
as a result of inbreeding are generally more prone to
genetic problems, and compliance with God's commands
would lead to stronger and healthier children.

The close relatives that a man could not marry can be
seen in the following diagram (Leviticus 18:6-17):

PROHIBITED RELATIONSHIPS IN ISRAEL			
Parents' generation	*Same generation*	*Childrens' generation*	*Grandchildrens' generation*
Aunt (12,13)	Half-sister (9)		
Mother (7)	Sister (9)	?	Grand-daughter (10)
Stepmother (8)	Stepsister (11)	Stepdaughter (17)	Stepgrand-daughter (11)
Aunt by marriage (14)	Sister-in-law (16)	Daughter-in-law (15)	

Perverted Worship

As with the restrictions about where animals could be killed and sacrificed, so these restricted relationships challenged the prevalent idolatrous practices that were familiar to the Israelites from their sojourn in Egypt. The phrase "Thou shalt not approach unto ...", as found for example in Leviticus 18:19, mimics language that is also used about worship – statements such as "bring an offering", or "draw near" use the same Hebrew term, *qarab*. Sexual immorality of the grossest kind was usually an integral part of much idol worship in both Egypt and Canaan, with special prominence given to incestuous relationships. This was the spiritual reason why God instructed His people not to engage in sexual relationships with any "that is near of kin". The need for Israel to be separate from idolatrous practices and pagan obsessions with blood also explains why (in addition to any hygienic concerns) it was forbidden for an Israelite to approach a woman "as long as she is put apart for her uncleanness" (Leviticus 18:19).

The diagram of restricted sexual relationships reveals a surprising omission. One of the 'first degree' blood relationships is the one between parent and child, yet there appears to be nothing to prevent a man from "approaching unto" his daughter. Ironically, however, this apparent omission only strengthens the case for viewing the commands as measures that prevented Israel from engaging in idolatry. In many parts of the Middle East where immorality and idolatry were rife, sexual relations between father and daughter were viewed as totally unacceptable. It was not therefore necessary to include this restriction, for it was already forbidden, even by pagan worshippers.*

Blood Relationship and Affinity

Forbidden relationships in Israel were determined on the basis of two main principles: blood relationship, and close

---

* Some commentators, however, point to the considerable moral laxity in Egypt, and believe that prohibition in the case of fathers and daughters was originally in verse 10, but was omitted at some stage by a copyist. There is no manuscript evidence for this view.

affinity through marriage. Sexual intercourse was forbidden between blood relatives of the first degree (a man's mother or sister) or of the second degree (his aunt or granddaughter). As well as these restrictions based on consanguinity, a man could not marry anyone closely related to him by marriage, such as his sister-in-law or his half-sister.

Three separate descriptions are used in Leviticus 18 to describe sexual relationships in addition to the phrase "approach unto", which has already been discussed. First, in verse 8, is the term, "to uncover nakedness", with its overtones of the shame of Adam and Eve when they sinned (cp. Genesis 3:7; Exodus 20:26; 28:42); secondly, "to lie with", which is used specifically in Leviticus 18 with reference not only to unlawful sexual relations, but also to ones that are perverse: i.e., homosexuality and bestiality (Leviticus 18:22,23). Thirdly, there is the word "take" – Hebrew, *laqach*, as in verses 17,18 – meaning to possess. This range of terms covers every eventuality, indicating that the passage refers to every form of sexual relationship: from casual promiscuity to formal marriage, and from unlawful relationships to ones that are perverted.

As if incestuous relationships were not abominable enough on their own, the Egyptians and Canaanites engaged in other abominations, and these were also denied to any Israelite who sought to uphold God's commands. For example, a man was not to commit adultery with his neighbour's wife (verse 20). This may not seem to be specially associated with idolatry, but it forms part of a set of commands from God that clearly identify idolatrous practices. This can be seen from a review of the additional commands that follow the list of restricted relationships. Israelites were not to:

1. lie with a woman in her impurity (verse 19)
2. take a neighbour's wife (verse 20)
3. offer children to idols (verse 21)
4. commit homosexuality (verse 22)
5. commit bestiality (verse 23)

Child Sacrifice

Central to this group of commands is the one prohibiting child sacrifice. Its appearance in this chapter probably indicates that there was also a sexual aspect to this abominable practice, showing the absolute degradation and perversity involved in false worship. Those who submitted to these practices believed that the gods would be appeased if children passed through the fire to Molech, and that the idolatrous deities welcomed perverted sexual activity. Nothing could be further from the purity and holiness demanded by Israel's God. Even the land itself is pictured as reacting in horror to the utter depravity of these practices:

"Defile not ye yourselves in any of these things: for in all these the nations are defiled which I cast out before you: *and the land is defiled*: therefore I do visit the iniquity thereof upon it, and the land itself vomiteth out her inhabitants." (verses 24,25)

By listing the behaviour that God would punish, Leviticus chapters 17 and 18 paint a vivid picture of the problems caused by idolatry. It is probably the most complete guide to those abominable practices anywhere in God's word, making it apparent that idolatrous behaviour was endemic in both Egypt and Canaan. It had been a serious problem when Israel dwelt in Egypt, and God sought to warn His people of the dangers lying ahead of them in the land of Canaan. Because idol worship is so sensual, it is attractive to the flesh and was not easily rooted out of the children of Israel, who managed somehow to keep a foot in both camps. In the New Testament, Stephen quoted words originally recorded by the prophet Amos to show that Israel mixed the worship of God with devotion to pagan gods:

"O ye house of Israel, have ye offered to me slain beasts and sacrifices by the space of forty years in the wilderness? Yea, ye took up the tabernacle of Moloch, and the star of your god Remphan, figures which ye made to worship them." (Acts 7:42,43; Amos 5:25-27)

Moloch (Molech) and Remphan were gods worshipped by many nations. Remphan is the name the Egyptians gave to the god Chiun (i.e., Saturn), whom the Syrians called

129

Rimmon, the star god (2 Kings 5:18). Molech, meaning king, is the Ammonite name for the god known elsewhere as Mars.

The Jerusalem Conference

The continuing belief in these gods in the first century created problems when Gentiles were converted to Christianity, and some Jewish believers therefore insisted that every male convert should be circumcised (Acts 15:1). The issue threatened to divide the first century ecclesias, and only the deliberations of the apostles at the Jerusalem conference averted outright schism. The conclusion reached by the apostles was to reconfirm God's message as given in Leviticus 17 and 18. Like Israel of old, members of the first century ecclesias were to forsake the gods of the surrounding nations and to try living holy lives:

> "It seemed good to the Holy Spirit, and to us, to lay upon you no greater burden than these necessary things; that ye abstain from meats offered to idols, and from blood, and from things strangled, and from fornication: from which if ye keep yourselves, ye shall do well." (Acts 15:28,29)

By saying that "it seemed good to the Holy Spirit, and to us", the Apostle James indicated that the principles evident in God's dealing with His people in the past still govern His people today. The apostles saw in these passages in Leviticus important guidelines relevant to the situation facing the first century ecclesias. Would believers be beguiled by pagan idolatry, and compromise their worship by trying to serve both God and mammon? God did not wish new converts to adopt the Law of Moses, because Christ came to fulfil the law. However, in order to show that they had left paganism behind, the apostles advised them to refrain from certain practices that were offensive to their Jewish brethren: their food was not to be meat that had been defiled through being offered to idols (see Leviticus 17:3,4), or killed by strangling – the method used in idolatrous sacrifices (see verse 13); they were to refrain from consuming blood like idol worshippers (see verses 10,14); and they should not engage in any sensual, adulterous or sexually perverted worship (see 18:6-23). The apostles thereby confirmed that holy living is as

130

necessary under Christ as it was when the nation lived in Canaan.

Be Ye Holy

This section in Leviticus therefore became an important passage for the apostles. But although the underlying principles of holiness still applied, the outcome of the Jerusalem conference was not to be treated as if it was simply updating Old Testament legislation. Life under Christ is radically different from life under the Law of Moses. In two of his epistles, therefore, Paul quotes from Leviticus 18:5 to show that the provisions of the law were all about external matters:

> "For Moses describeth the righteousenss which is of the law, That the man which doeth those things shall live by them."
> (Romans 10:5)

In this passage the emphasis is on the word "doeth". It is therefore apparent, he says, that "the law is not of faith" (Galatians 3:12), and that there is a "righteousness which is of faith" (Romans 10:6).

Believers in Christ are not governed by laws that say "touch not, taste not, handle not". Such regulations, says Paul, "lack any value in restraining sensual indulgence" (Colossians 2:23, NIV). God's appeal is to be holy, like unto Him. Separation is more a matter of drawing near to God than of erecting barriers against the pressures of the world. These chapters in Leviticus are therefore also valuable for us if they cause us to examine our own lives to see what compromises we may have made with the modern world and its idolatry. For God has said, "Ye shall be holy: for I the LORD your God am holy" (Leviticus 19:2).

131

18

CRIME AND PUNISHMENT
Leviticus 19,20

AFTER all the details earlier in Leviticus about sacrifices and offerings, the appointment and duties of the priests, clean and unclean food, disease and uncleanness, the Day of Atonement, and the problem of idolatry, the subjects in chapters 19 and 20 seem to have no obvious theme. In fact some Bibles call them a "Repetition of sundry laws", as if there is no special order or purpose behind the collection and it is simply a miscellany of unrelated regulations. Yet careful reading soon indicates that there is a strong structure and pattern centring on the most important verse in the whole book: "Ye shall be holy: for I the LORD your God am holy" (19:2). This verse is expanded at the end of chapter 20 to explain that the holiness God seeks from His people will involve them not only drawing near to Him in order to learn His ways, but also in the process separating themselves from the ungodliness of other nations: "Ye shall be holy unto me: for I the LORD am holy, and have severed you from other people, that ye should be mine" (20:26).

Chapter 19 reflects on the ten commandments and connects them to the great truth, "I am the LORD your God". God Himself was impressing upon Israel the need for personal and national holiness, and this important statement becomes a refrain throughout the chapter, dividing it into separate sections. These sections, all concluding with either "I am the LORD your God" or "I am the LORD" are listed in the table facing. Where they refer specifically to one of the ten commandments, this is indicated in the third column.

The different subjects in Leviticus 19 also fall into three groups, as indicated in the right hand column of the table:
- verses 3-10, relating to God
- verses 11-18, relating to neighbours
- verses 19-37, the problems of compromise

ANALYSIS OF LEVITICUS 19			
Honour parents & the sabbath	verse 3	IV, V	Relating to God
Shun idolatry	verse 4	I, II	
All food is God's	verses 5-10		
Live honestly	verses 11,12	VIII, IX, III	Relating to neighbours
No exploitation	verses 13,14	VIII	
Righteous judgement	verses 15,16	VI, IX	
Love your neighbour	verses 17,18	X	
No mixed breeding	verses 19-25	VII	No compromising with the world
No pagan practices	verses 26-28		
No sacred prostitution	verses 29,30	VII	
No necromancy	verse 31		
Show respect for age	verse 32		
Love the stranger	verses 33,34		
Upright in business	verses 35-37		

Relating to God

The first of these sections commences by bringing together the family duty of parental respect and the divine observance of God's sanctified day, the sabbath (Leviticus 19:3). Clearly, in God's sight, the two are inseparable, and they establish the foundation for a life of holiness. The pursuit of holiness has therefore to begin in the home. For children, parents stand in place of God; and through their care and instruction children should learn about God and about His ways. This was also the Apostle's message in Hebrews 12:9: "Furthermore we have had fathers of our flesh which corrected us, and we gave them reverence: shall we not much rather be in subjection unto the Father of spirits, and live?"

Holiness in the family and in the home concerning earthly things has also to translate into holiness in a person's spiritual life, and this begins with observing God's sabbath where the focus is on divine issues, not human ones. The natural consequence of hallowing the sabbath is to turn away from idols – literally "things of nought" (Leviticus 19:4).

The last part of the section dealing with issues relating to God (verses 5-10) looks at two consequences of drawing closer to Him. First, it deals with freewill peace offerings, explaining that they could not be consumed on or after the third day. Mention of "the third day" suggests hygienic considerations that also have a spiritual significance. Holiness is the antithesis of corruption, and corruption sets in after the third day, as Lazarus' sister Martha indicated (John 11:39). Therefore, in their offerings Israelites were to remember they were approaching a holy and incorruptible God, who could be approached only as He determined. When they did follow God's directions, He was gracious to them, and they shared their meal with Him in fellowship. After all, He had provided the food, and it came from His storehouse.

These thoughts link directly with the second consequence of drawing closer to God, which at first may appear to have no direct connection. But it is connected as strongly as respect for parents is linked with honouring the sabbath. God instructed farmers to make provision during harvest time "for the poor and the stranger": gleanings were to be left for them in the field and vineyard. The message was clear: God provides food for all, and as His children we must not stand by while others go hungry. The same lesson, but in a New Testament context, occurs in 1 Corinthians 11, where brethren and sisters were criticised for feasting while others went hungry. The Apostle had to say: "despise ye the church of

God, and shame them that have not?" (1 Corinthians 11:22).

Relating to Neighbours

An appreciation of God and His ways should affect a person's behaviour towards his neighbour. The next section therefore includes the third commandment about not taking God's name in vain (Leviticus 19:12, cp. Exodus 20:7), but surrounds it by commands about how to act properly towards others by not stealing, lying or cheating. Such behaviour is an outright denial of God's name. Any thought of exploitation should also be put aside; the poor should not be oppressed, and the underprivileged should be treated compassionately, for does not the Lord God show boundless compassion? He is also a righteous judge who cannot be influenced, so His people must be upright when disputes have to be settled; they should not engage in a campaign of malicious gossip, or refuse to get involved when a neighbour's life is endangered.

Godly behaviour towards others will be easier if grudges and differences are not allowed to grow or fester. The main aim should therefore be to "love thy neighbour as thyself". This "Royal Law", as the Apostle James termed it (James 2:8), was therefore often quoted by the Lord Jesus as the ideal for which his followers should strive (Matthew 19:19; 22:39; Mark 12:31; Luke 10:27).

Holiness in Practice

The third section of Leviticus 19 appears particularly to be just a collection of miscellaneous commands. Yet they are all related to the main theme of the chapter whereby the Israelites were being taught how to practise holiness in their everyday lives. There is an implicit warning against compromise with the people of the land whose ways were totally out of step with the things of Israel's God. By forbidding the mingling of different fibres in clothing, different plant seeds in a field, and different cattle when breeding, God's people were shown the importance of faithfully following His ways, for with God there is "never the slightest variation or shadow of inconsistency" (James 1:17, J B Phillips).

A different form of unacceptable mingling occurred if a man consorted with a slave woman who was betrothed to another man. In all other societies of the time, slaves were regarded as possessions to be used without thought of the consequences. Whereas under other circumstances adultery or fornication merited death, in this case the woman was not completely free. However, the man was also not free to act as he wished, and he had to acknowledge his offence by bringing a trespass offering – he had sinned against the woman and her future husband (Leviticus 19:20-22).

As God's people, the Israelites were not to rush to obtain fruit from newly planted trees, but allow them to become established for three years, and devote the fourth year's harvest to God before using the fruit for themselves: "that it may yield unto you the increase thereof" (verse 25). The trees represented the Israelites who were entering the land; they were to become firmly established and devoted to God if they were to increase and bring forth good fruit. By showing these qualities of patience, devotion and care as children of God, the people would align themselves with Israel's God, and not with the idolatrous gods of Canaan or Egypt. Practices associated with idolatry were therefore to be shunned completely – eating blood, engaging in sorcery, making marks on the body or shaving the hair or beard. Because of the gross immorality associated with pagan idolatry, God also warned against the practices of prostitution, necromancy and wizardry. Any involvement in these would be an affront to God and His sanctuary.

The chapter concludes with regulations about displaying the proper attitude of respect towards the rest of mankind: honour for those who are older, care for those from other nations, and integrity in business (verses 32-37). Any other form of behaviour is incompatible with the divine qualities God reveals. If we respect and reverence the Creator, He asks that we also show respect and care for His creatures.

Leviticus 20

In order for laws to be effective as deterrents against crime there must be serious consequences for those who offend against them. Leviticus 20 thus lists offences that carried the death sentence in Israel, so seriously were they regarded as sins against both God and society. The list was essentially as follows:

1. Engaging in idolatrous child sacrifices (verses 1-5)
2. Consulting with mediums and spiritualists (verse 6)
3. Practising witchcraft (verse 27)
4. Cursing parents (verse 9)
5. Committing adultery (verse 10)
6. Sexual relationships with close relatives (verses 11,12,17-21)
7. Practising homosexuality or bestiality (verses 13,15,16)

The fact that the list starts with pagan sacrifices shows that the purpose of the commands was to prevent Israel from adopting the idolatry that was common in both Egypt and Canaan. The most extreme and repulsive elements of pagan worship involved parents sacrificing their children to Molech, an allegedly insatiable deity, as well as all manner of perverted sexual practices. Molech is described in 1 Kings 11:7 as an Ammonite god, though it is possible that Molech worship, whether under that name or not, was first introduced in ancient Babylonia. The name "Molech" (sometimes Moloch, Milcom or Malcham) is a corruption of *melek*, meaning 'King'. It is apparent from Isaiah 57:5 and Jeremiah 19:5 that worship of Molech involved both the ritual killing and burning of children, though it is possible that it also involved a less extreme form of sacrifice, perhaps a 'trial by fire'. The punishment for sacrificing children to Molech was stoning – this method of execution was undertaken by "the people of the land" so that it would express the nation's rejection of the sin, and also act as a strong deterrent to others.

So serious was the crime of child sacrifice that anyone learning of it yet remaining silent would be "cut off". Whereas the stoning of an offender was the responsibility of the general population, God would act in the case of anyone who condoned the sin, and "cut him off from among his people" (Leviticus 20:5). The same punishment would befall any who consulted with spiritualist mediums, and thus condoned pagan practices (verse 6). The close association between the different crimes mentioned in

Leviticus 20 clearly indicates that worship of Molech involved, in addition to child sacrifice, magical arts, unlawful sexual perversions, and some form of profane swearing. Cursing parents was a crime equivalent to blasphemy. It was apparent from Leviticus 19:3 that parents stand in the same relation to their children as God does to His children. Children cursing their parents denies the respect that is due to them, and also denies their God-given role. The punishment for this blasphemy was death (20:9). So it was also for anyone who claimed to be a medium (verse 27).

For sexual sins there was a range of punishments. Death by stoning was reserved for the most serious cases: adultery, homosexuality and bestiality. Other offenders would be "cut off" by God; and yet others would "bear their sin; they shall die childless". In one case – when a man took both a woman and her mother as wives – "it is wickedness: they shall be burnt with fire" (verse 14). Here the method of pagan sacrifice was used ironically as the form of punishment for anyone who offended in this way, suggesting that this was a crime specifically associated with idolatrous worship. The emphasis in this section on incestuous sins is also very appropriate once it is realised that all the listed crimes stemmed originally from worship of Molech "the abomination of the Ammonites", for Ammon and Moab were born as a result of the incestuous relationship between Lot and his two daughters (Genesis 19:36).

19

TO WHOM MUCH IS GIVEN
Leviticus 21,22

AFTER reminding the people of their need to remain separate from the idolatrous ways of the Canaanites, God told Moses to give instructions to "the priests the sons of Aaron" (Leviticus 21:1). The underlying message was the same for the priests as it was for the people: the land had been defiled by the abominations of the Canaanites, who were being dispossessed for their iniquity; so woe betide anyone in Israel who followed those evil ways. As for the people, so for the priests, the aim was holiness:

"They shall be holy unto their God, and not profane the name of their God: for the offerings of the LORD made by fire, and the bread of their God, they do offer: therefore they shall be holy." (verse 6, cp. 19:2; 20:7)

The motivation was also to be the same: God is holy, and therefore His people must be holy too.

The separation required of priests, and especially of the high priest, however, was even more stringent than for the people. The priesthood in general, and the high priest in particular, were in the position of representing God to the nation. Their whole life was to be associated with holy things, and because "unto whomsoever much is given, of him shall be much required" (Luke 12:48), the issues of holiness and separation were even more demanding in their case. The holiness described in Leviticus chapters 21 and 22 covered ritual observances, but these were clearly intended to translate into holiness of character and behaviour. The recurring phrase in chapters 18–20 was "I am the LORD your God"; in its fullest form in chapters 21 and 22 it is "I the LORD, which sanctify you, am holy" (21:8; see also 21:15,23; 22:16,32).

Perfection for priests

This phrase separates into five parts the chapters addressed to the priests, just as the similar phrase divided the chapters addressed to the people. These sections are set out below, in a clearly chiastic pattern:

A. Priests were not to defile themselves by contact with the death of anyone outside their immediate family, or by marrying a profane woman (21:1-8).

    B. The high priest was not to be defiled by contact with the death of anybody, including his close family; he was to marry only a virgin "of his own people" (21:10-15).

        C. Priests were not to have any physical imperfections (21:16-23).

    B. Priests were not to minister at the tabernacle if they were defiled – by leprosy, an issue, or contact with death (22:1-16).

A. Priests were not to accept any blemished offerings, any animals less than a week old, or any animal and its young on the same day (22:17-33).

The more onerous responsibilities of the sons of Aaron are epitomised by the requirement occupying the central position in the above list. All members of the priesthood were to be completely free from any physical defect: "no man that hath a blemish of the seed of Aaron the priest shall come nigh to offer the offerings of the LORD made by fire" (21:21). Under the law, physical perfection was emblematic of moral perfection, so that the people were instructed to bring offerings to the priests that were also spotless: "whatsoever hath a blemish, that shall ye not offer, for it shall not be acceptable for you" (22:20). The person bringing the offering was thus declaring that, despite his failure to achieve it, his aim and direction was the pursuit of holiness, perfection, obedience and commitment. The need for such an offering emphasised his personal inadequacy, and his desire to draw ever closer to God. There was also a responsibility for the priests to ensure they did not accept any offering that was less than physically perfect (22:20-25).

Natural sympathy causes us to think about the effect of this legislation upon any blemished or disabled descendants of Aaron who were barred from the priesthood through no personal or moral cause. Were they simply cast aside? Though the scriptures do not specifically comment on their circumstances, similar restrictions were not placed on other members of the tribe of Levi and it is probable that general levitical duties could be fulfilled by descendants of Aaron who were not able to be priests.

Defiled by contact with death

The lessons of defilement in daily life, taught so powerfully to the nation of Israel by the regulations under the law relating to clean and unclean foods, and by the arrangements to prevent contamination by sin, disease, and death, also translated into practical controls that affected the priests. Take, for example, defilement by death. Priests were to ensure that they kept away from all contact with dead bodies (21:1). There was some leniency in this command where a close relative was involved – father, mother, son, daughter, brother or unmarried sister – and this most probably referred to any funeral arrangements for these family members. Because of the compassionate leniency of the law in these circumstances, the command to Ezekiel "the priest" not to mourn even when his wife died (Ezekiel 24:15-18) would shock all who knew the details of the law.

But this was the position of any descendant of Aaron who became the nation's *high* priest. Because he had been anointed, wore the consecrated garments, and appeared before God on the people's behalf, the high priest was not allowed to mourn, even for his close relatives (Leviticus 21:10-12). It is apparent that this restriction applied only because of the office he held and not through any personal holiness. The high priest symbolised the great High Priest who was to come, over whom death no longer has any dominion. He also symbolised the hopes and aspirations of God's people finally to be free from the restrictions of sin and death. In his behaviour were to be seen the principles to which every Israelite was taught to aspire.

141

Increasing requirements
The different requirements that applied to the people, to the priests, and then to the high priest must not be regarded as a lack of consistency on God's part. The differences were necessary to declare that the requirement for holiness increases the nearer a person draws to God. Only Levites were allowed to enter and serve at the tabernacle, so the other Israelites had less onerous restrictions placed upon them. The levitical priests, because they served in holy things on behalf of their brother Israelites, were required to display in visible ways the holiness that God requires. Yet God is merciful, and He allowed some relaxation in the requirements relating to defilement by contact with dead bodies when a member of a priest's family died. The high priest, however, who alone had the privilege of entering into the Most Holy Place to serve before God's glory, was to remain ritually undefiled as a constant reminder to the people of God's intrinsic holiness.

The Apostle Paul declared that "the law was our schoolmaster to bring us unto Christ" (Galatians 3:24), and there can be no doubt that the strictures affecting the priests and the high priest also had that objective. There were regulations, for example, about who they could and could not marry. Priests could not marry a prostitute or anyone who was considered profane – i.e., guilty of immorality (Leviticus 21:7). The high priest's choice was even more limited: "he shall take a wife in her virginity" (verses 13,14). These restrictions all looked forward to the High Priest to come, of whom it is written that "virgins … follow the Lamb whithersoever he goeth" (Revelation 14:4). The ritual teaching therefore contained a vital spiritual message.

As it was a requirement that the priests and the high priest should enter into exemplary marriages, the children of priests were to appreciate that their behaviour could also reflect adversely upon their parents' role and responsibilities. So if a priest's daughter became a prostitute she was to be "burnt with fire" (Leviticus 21:9) as an exemplary warning to all. Prostitution was such an integral part of idol worship that an example needed to be

142

set if anyone closely associated with the worship of Israel's God became involved. Even the form of punishment in this case was significant. Most of the serious crimes in Israel were punished by stoning. Burning was commanded in this case as a salutary reminder of the abominable human sacrifices offered to Molech as part of the immoral and idolatrous worship of that false god (see also 20:14 and comments on page 138).

Privileges lead to sanctification

Though a priest's family had to be careful not to bring shame on him through their behaviour, there were also great benefits that came from their relationship to him. They shared his portion of "the holy thing" – the food reserved for the priests from the peace offerings given by the people (22:10-16). This too was symbolic. Much better than the holy food of the sacrifices was the holy food of God's word. The priest had a responsibility to teach this to the people, "and they should seek the law at his mouth" (Malachi 2:7); undoubtedly he also had a responsibility to teach it to his family.

These principles of holiness that applied to the priests carry through into New Testament teaching for those who wish to be kings and priests in the kingdom age. Ecclesias should appoint as elders, for example, only those who are not compromised by the behaviour of their wives or families (1 Timothy 3:11,12; Titus 1:6). Balancing these greater requirements are the special advantages that can flow from believers' families being exposed regularly to holy things. The Apostle Paul therefore wrote to the Corinthians who were troubled by brethren and sisters who had unbelieving partners, and reassured them that "the unbelieving husband is sanctified by the wife, and the unbelieving wife is sanctified by the husband: else were your children unclean; but now are they holy" (1 Corinthians 7:14). This passage uses Leviticus vocabulary, with words like "sanctified", "unclean" and "holy".

By comparing the Old and New Testament passages it is apparent that the sanctification Paul mentions arises from a believer's family becoming exposed to "holy things". The believer brings to marriage a different attitude of mind: one that is selfless and sacrificial, and the

143

unbelieving partner should become the greatest beneficiary of this Christlike attitude. Children of believers – even when one parent is an unbeliever – are raised in the nurture and admonition of the Lord and, because of their regular exposure to the good things of God, they are able to make an informed decision when they reach the age of responsibility.

The same situation must have applied to priestly and levitical families in Old Testament times. Because service at the tabernacle and temple was restricted to the tribe of Levi it was important that levitical children were instructed from an early age in the things of God. What was necessary for practical reasons within Levi was valuable for spiritual reasons in all other tribes, which is why parents were encouraged to remember God's commandments:

> "Thou shalt teach them diligently unto thy children … and thou shalt write them upon the posts of thy house, and on thy gates."   (Deuteronomy 6:6-9)

Uncleanness separates from God

We might conclude from these special regulations for the sons of Aaron that the priests were different from others in Israel. Yet they were just as liable to be defiled, however conscientiously they approached each part of their lives. Ritual defilement could occur at any time, and the Day of Atonement recognised that there was need for reconciliation even for the most diligent member of the nation. If any priest was unclean through leprosy, issue or contact with a dead body, he should immediately separate himself from all priestly tasks, or else bring shame on God's holy name. Priests stood in the same relationship to God as their wives and families did to them. As so often in Leviticus, the message was clear that uncleanness, however it might arise, is defiling, and separates man from God.

SUMMARY OF THE LAW OF HOLINESS
(Leviticus chapters 17–22)

- To prevent Israel descending into idolatry, no animals could be slain for food unless they were first offered in sacrifice to God
- Because of the rampant sexual immorality associated with pagan worship, Israel was instructed to refrain from incestuous unions
- The repulsive practice of child sacrifice, common among the Canaanite people, was not to feature in Israel's worship
- Idolatry, blood sacrifices, and fornication were still abhorrent to God in New Testament times (Acts 15)
- Israel was not only to refrain from idolatry, but actively to practise holiness by adopting the divine character
- Serious breaches of the law of holiness were to be punished by death – usually by stoning, but occasionally by fire as a parody of pagan sacrifice
- Greater demands of holiness were required from priests, the sons of Aaron, because of their closeness to the things of God
- For the high priest, who was closest of all, the conditions were particularly onerous
- Priests and the high priest were to be physically without blemish, indicating that true holiness requires a similar degree of moral perfection
- Priests' families were to be beyond reproach; in return they benefited from sharing the sacrificial meals and other "holy things"

20

THE CALENDAR
Leviticus 23

THE annual religious calendar kept to the fore the need for men and women in Israel to practise holiness every day of their lives. Certain aspects of the calendar are an integral part of the "Law of Holiness" as we have called Leviticus chapters 18–27. Like earlier sections of the Law of Holiness, the section dealing with details about the calendar is structured by the repetition of the phrase "I am the LORD your God" (Leviticus 23:22,43). The phrase marks out distinct subsections, as well as giving the reason why every individual Israelite should seek after holiness. These subsections are shown below:

ISRAEL'S RELIGIOUS YEAR		
23:1-3	Introduction, the weekly sabbath	
23:4-22	The Spring-time festivals	
	4-14	Passover & Unleavened Bread
	15-22	Feast of Weeks
23:23-44	The Autumn festivals	
	23-32	Feast of Trumpets & Day of Atonement
		Feast of Tabernacles

Significant phrases

It is apparent from this table that Leviticus 23 is not a complete record of the religious calendar; there is no mention, for example, of the daily sacrifices that were offered every morning and evening, or of the festival of the new moon. There are three other recurring phrases in chapter 23, and these focus attention on the chapter's main objective. The first of these phrases – "the feasts of the LORD" – is sometimes translated "appointed seasons of the LORD" (see 23:2, RV margin), or more simply "the

REPEATED PHRASES IN LEVITICUS 23	
Feasts of the LORD	verses 2,4,37,44
Holy convocations	verses 2,4,7,8,21,24,27,35,37
Ye shall do no (servile) work	verses 7,8,21,25,28,30,31,36

LORD's meetings" (G J Wenham, *The Book of Leviticus*). Although the feasts were occasions when Israelites congregated together, as another phrase explains, the prime purpose of every feast was that each individual Israelite should meet God. They were His feasts, His gatherings, His meetings.

Only in a secondary sense therefore were the feasts occasions for Israelites to meet each other, and the phrase used to describe this aspect is qualified so that the primary purpose of their meetings could not be overlooked. They were to be "holy convocations", gatherings, conventions or assemblies. They were "holy" assemblies because the people were called to meet in consciousness of God's presence. Emphasising the holy and separate nature of these assemblies, the next repeated phrase forbade the people from engaging in any of their normal daily activities: "ye shall do no servile work" (or, "work of labour", verse 7, RV margin). They were to be strictly days of "solemn rest" (verse 3, RV): days when man ceased from his labours as God ceased from His on the seventh day of creation.

The spiritual significance of the sabbath underlies every aspect of these assemblies, and this is indicated by the emphasis throughout the year on the number seven. The sabbath was every seventh day, and the feasts often extended to seven days. There was increased spiritual activity during the seventh month, when most of the festivals occurred. Throughout the year there were a total of seven days of solemn rest (in addition to the weekly sabbath):

1. First day Unleavened bread
2. Seventh day Unleavened bread
3. Weeks
4. Trumpets

5. Day of Atonement
6. First day Tabernacles
7. Day after Tabernacles

As if this was not sufficient to impress on Israel the great truth that God was inviting them into His eternal rest, every seventh year was a sabbatical year, and the seventh seventh-year was a super-sabbath year called the Jubilee.* How could anyone in Israel miss the point that was being made? Even if the weekly sabbath became commonplace and lost its significance, the interruption of daily life by the other annual gatherings would surely show that God was calling His people to rest with Him, as the Lord Jesus invites his disciples: "Come unto me, all ye that labour and are heavy laden, and I will give you rest" (Matthew 11:28).

The sabbath template

The sabbath therefore prepared the Israelites for the special days of holy convocation, and established a template for their lives as people serving a Holy God. The other days of holy convocation were often referred to as special sabbaths: see, for example, how the Day of Atonement is described in the following passage:

"It shall be unto you a sabbath of rest, and ye shall afflict your souls: in the ninth day of the month at even, from even unto even, shall ye celebrate your sabbath."
(Leviticus 23:32)

This was particularly true of the Day of Atonement. For whereas it was commanded on the days of holy convocation that the Israelites should not engage in any servile work, on sabbath days and on the Day of Atonement no work at all was allowed:

"In it thou shalt not do any work, thou, nor thy son, nor thy daughter, thy manservant, nor thy maidservant, nor thy cattle, nor thy stranger that is within thy gates."
(Exodus 20:10)

Not even a fire could be kindled (35:3).

* Details of these special years appear in Leviticus 25. See chapter 22, page 161.

On the other days of holy convocation, some work was allowed even though all "servile" work was banned. Servile work was labour associated with a person's worldly calling: the farmer could not plough, and the smith could not work at his forge. But meals could be prepared, as on any other day, and presumably a fire could be kindled to cook the meal:

> "There shall be an holy convocation to you; no manner of work shall be done in them, save that which every man must eat, that only may be done of you."
>
> (Exodus 12:16)

Local assemblies

Although holy convocations were gatherings of the people to concentrate on remembering God's holiness and mercy, we must not assume that they all took place at the national sanctuary. Such attendances were required only on three occasions during the year, at the feast of Unleavened Bread, at Pentecost and at Tabernacles (Exodus 23:14-17). The other occasions were to be celebrated locally, and probably were intended to reflect the attitudes, devotion and respect that were shown during the three so-called "pilgrim feasts".* They would also help to bind all Israelites into the system of national worship, and not just "all thy males".

The days that were thus set apart were made available for religious purposes and were probably held in every town and village once the nation had entered the promised land. Indeed, it may well have been the memory of these gatherings that caused the exiles to institute the synagogue gatherings that formed such a major part of Jewish life once they were back in the land. The New Testament word "synagogue" means congregation or assembly and is virtually synonymous with "convocation", though the latter word has the additional meaning of being called to assemble together. A similar meaning attaches to another New Testament word "ecclesia", which carries the idea of being called forth to assemble together, usually with the objective of engaging in religious

---

* The Hebrew word for these feasts, *chag*, is the same Arabic word *haj* used to describe the pilgrimages to Mecca.

149

activities. This explains the importance for today's disciples of what was arranged for the people of God in Old Testament times, causing us to consider the underlying principles about communal worship.

Because the term "sabbath" literally means to cease or to rest, it is easy to view the concept negatively as an occasion when men and women in Israel were prevented from doing what they desired. Its object was wholly different, however. God intervened in the inexorable and constant round of toil that was man's lot from the day Adam sinned, and showed him what lies in store for His people. Because of His love for Israel, this message was reinforced by the days of holy convocation and the feasts that were held every year.

Passover and Unleavened Bread

After describing the sabbath, the rest of Leviticus 23 follows the order of the religious calendar. The first annual event was Passover, treated here as separate from the feast of Unleavened Bread. The two days of holy convocation are actually associated with Unleavened Bread and not with Passover, but it seems that the distinction between Passover and Unleavened Bread was soon lost and the two names were used interchangeably. Passover also provides a template for later celebrations. It was clearly an occasion when the message of redemption and deliverance from Egypt was reinforced within each family unit (Exodus 12:26-28), and subsequent feasts were also opportunities for religious instruction and celebration. The nation's unique history could be recounted, and lessons drawn out for the special circumstances that were being faced by those who gathered together to worship, just as we do today with exhortations and studies based on the scriptures.

Passover celebrated God's power in taking His people out of Egypt. Subsequent feasts celebrated the same power revealed in the passing seasons of seedtime and harvest. The celebration of firstfruits emphasised that God who brought the infant nation into the land with the intention that His people would be fruitful and become a great harvest, also ensured that the firstfruits of their natural harvest promised full storehouses when all was safely gathered in.

New Testament teaching

The importance of the firstfruits is emphasised by New Testament teaching, but must have been understood to some degree by thoughtful and faithful Israelites. The Apostle Paul spoke of the charge he received to preach the Gospel:

> "How that Christ died for our sins according to the scriptures; and that he was buried, and that he rose again the third day according to the scriptures."
>
> (1 Corinthians 15:3,4)

One of the scriptures pointing to the Lord's resurrection on "the third day" is Leviticus 23:11, where the sheaf of firstfruits was waved "before the LORD ... on the morrow after the sabbath". The sabbath referred to here was the holy convocation at the beginning of the feast of Unleavened Bread, making "the morrow after the sabbath" the third day after Passover.

There may also be a reference to this in Luke's account of Jesus' disciples plucking ears of corn on the sabbath day. This incident occurred on "the second sabbath after the first" (Luke 6:1), and provided a basis for Jesus to teach his critics that "the Son of man is Lord also of the sabbath" (verse 5), meaning that the sabbath and all that it signified found fulfilment in him.

A similar foreshadowing of greater things in Israel's calendar occurred later in the religious year. Seven sabbaths after the Christ-sheaf was waved before God, two loaves were waved at Pentecost. They too were called "firstfruits unto the LORD" (Leviticus 23:17), and represented how both Jews and Gentiles become the eventual harvest of the Lord's work. Because these spiritual lessons are about God's people more than about His land, the chapter includes a short section reminding the Israelites to make provision for the poor and the stranger by leaving corn for gleaning in the corners of their fields. This reminder about the needy concludes with the message, "I am the LORD your God" (verse 22). Could the message be clearer? God always cares for the poor and needy. He did so when He took Israel out of Egypt, and when He cared for them in the wilderness. His message of salvation was to sinners, not to the righteous. If the Israelites understood this, they were to show it by acting as He acted. It was the implicit demand of His holiness.

Harvest home

The spiritual harvest and the great day of rest when God's storehouse is filled is the picture described in Leviticus 23. The chapter ends with the festival of greatest rejoicing, what the farmer calls harvest home: "Ye shall rejoice before the LORD your God seven days" (verse 40). The emphasis on the number seven which has already been noted is inescapable here. The Israelites were to rejoice seven days; the feast was to be kept seven days, and celebrated in the seventh month; throughout the feast they were to dwell in booths seven days to remember the great deliverance from Egypt (verses 39-44).

These activities were intended to bind God's people closer to Him and closer to each other. In the process they learned of God's holiness, and were encouraged to greater holiness themselves. Some words written many generations later neatly summarise the message of Leviticus 23:

"Let us consider one another to provoke unto love and to good works: not forsaking the assembling of ourselves together, as the manner of some is; but exhorting one another: and so much the more, as ye see the day approaching." (Hebrews 10:24,25)

152

21

DAILY DEVOTION
Leviticus 24

THE information in Leviticus 23 about the religious calendar, continues in chapter 25 with details of the year of release and the jubilee. But the record of feasts and observances is interrupted by details in chapter 24 about the lampstand, the table of showbread and the case of a man who blasphemed God's name. Commentators do not agree why this interruption occurs. Those who follow the nineteenth century higher critics say the material comes from different original sources; but this does not satisfactorily answer why the information about the calendar is interrupted. No editor would disrupt material so strongly linked by a common theme purely because he had other material from another source on a different subject. As believers in divine inspiration, we must look for another explanation as to why God interrupted the theme of the national calendar.

Some commentators think that the details of the lampstand and table of showbread were introduced at this stage to reinforce the fact that there were *daily* religious ordinances in addition to the periodical holy convocations mentioned in chapter 24. While this could be a reason for including information about the lampstand and the showbread, it does not explain why the incident of the blasphemous man is also included here. Before seeing if there is a common theme in chapter 24 to explain why it has been inserted at this point, it may be helpful first of all to ask why the information about the calendar has been divided into two, with some details appearing in chapter 23 and the rest in chapter 25.

As we have seen, chapter 23 is concerned with holy convocations: the periodic occasions during the year when opportunity was provided to cease from daily tasks and join together with other Israelites to remember God's constant goodness. The aspects of the calendar recorded in chapter 25 were not holy convocations. They were, it is true, extensions of the sabbath pattern – the year of release occurred every seventh year, and the jubilee was celebrated every seventh year of release. But although each of these sabbatical years had its quota of holy convocations, they were no more numerous than in any other year.

The calendar as recorded in Leviticus was therefore in two distinct parts: occasions that were holy convocations, and occasions that were not. The message of these two parts combined to teach the need for holiness every day of an Israelite's life. The special days provided periodic opportunities to remember what God had done for the nation and for individuals, but this remembrance was also to be a continuing and daily influence with the hope of eventually sharing in an eternal rest. What better symbols could there be of the need to feed each day on God's word, and to devote daily labours to God, than the lampstand and the table of showbread? The need to be aware continually of God's presence also underlies the issue of the man who blasphemed. He had not elevated God in his heart or mind, and had no shame when he blasphemed the divine name. It was the antithesis of the holiness God demanded of His people.

Viewed in this way, Leviticus 24 does not interrupt the details of the religious calendar so much as bring together the two parts, and explain their special purpose.

Oil for the light

The details provided about the lampstand do not focus on the item of furniture, but only on the light it produced. One of the key words in Leviticus 24:1-4 is "continually". The lamps had to burn *continually* (verse 1), and the high priest was responsible for *continually* monitoring and maintaining the lamps (verses 2,3). The lamps were displayed "before the LORD *continually*", just as God promised always to be with His people. The reality and the symbol were therefore combined in this message about the lampstand.

The other key word in this passage is "pure". In order to create the conditions for a pure light, the Israelites were instructed to provide *"pure* olive oil"*.* Any impurity would be immediately obvious. There would be a guttering flame and smoke rather than clear bright light. To represent the purity of God's word, only the purest fuel was allowed. We are reminded of the well known words in Psalm 119: "Thy word is a lamp unto my feet, and a light unto my path" (Psalm 119:105).

One other aspect of the lampstand is mentioned in this short section. Though the lamps were to burn continually before the Lord, the lampstand was sited "without the vail of the testimony, in the tabernacle of the congregation" (Leviticus 24:3). This showed that the light was God's, but was for the benefit of His people, His congregation.

The showbread

The words used in connection with the lampstand also appear in the description of the showbread (verses 5-9). The loaves were to be "set in order before the LORD *continually"*, and placed on "the *pure* table", with *"pure* frankincense" as a memorial. The emphasis on continuity is explained by two further terms: the bread was placed on behalf of the children of Israel "by an *everlasting* covenant"; it was "a *perpetual* statute".* Like circumcision and the sabbath, the showbread symbolised God's covenant with Israel.

Symbols can express a number of different aspects, and thus are a sort of spiritual shorthand. This is particularly true of the showbread. First, bread is symbolic of human labour and man's mortality. Adam was told, "in the sweat of thy face shalt thou eat bread, till thou return unto the ground" (Genesis 3:19). By laying up the loaves before the Lord, the twelve tribes of Israel were acknowledging that God oversaw all their labour; it was important that they dedicated all they did to His service. Secondly, bread represents basic sustenance and the simplest meal. God gives us each day our daily bread (Matthew 6:11), and the loaves therefore represented the constant divine provision for man's returning needs. Through the frankincense

---

* Both "everlasting" and "perpetual" translate the Hebrew word *olam*, with its implicit sense of anticipating an eternal future that is currently hidden from view.

associated with the showbread, which was burnt on the altar of incense, God accepted and partook of the Israelites' offering. He was pleased with it, and thus He sanctified Israel's labour, sustaining them daily so that they could continually give Him pleasure.

The loaves were renewed every sabbath day (Leviticus 24:8), and the high priest and his sons, as God's representatives, ate the old loaves. It was therefore a sabbath day when David and his men fled from Saul and asked Ahimelech the priest for food, "for there was no bread there but the shewbread, that was taken from before the LORD, to put hot bread *in the day when it was taken away*" (1 Samuel 21:6). Knowing the restrictions of Leviticus 24, that the high priest and his sons should eat the bread "in a holy place", Ahimelech needed to know that David and his men were not ritually unclean. With the reassurance that "women have been kept from us about these three days, since I came out, and the vessels of the young men are holy" (verse 5), Ahimelech gave David the showbread. As they ate the bread David and his companions shared in the fellowship with God that was promised in His covenant with Israel.

The covenant brought great responsibilities. Every Israelite should dedicate himself completely to God – this was the labour that gave God pleasure. Also, because God's word was their guide, the people had a responsibility to witness to His truth. All this required dedication, devotion and a constant awareness of God's presence and holiness. Through his visit to the priests at Nob, David was reassured of God's nearness and protection.

The true message of the showbread was not always understood. Jesus had to explain to the Pharisees about the real purpose of the sabbath and the showbread, using David and his men as an example. The Pharisees complained about the disciples plucking ears of corn on a sabbath day, and Jesus had to rebuke them:

"Have ye not read what David did? ... If ye had known what this meaneth, I will have mercy, and not sacrifice, ye would not have condemned the guiltless.

For the Son of man is Lord even of the sabbath day."
(Matthew 12:3,7,8)

"Mercy and not sacrifice": this truth was taught by placing twelve loaves before the Lord God every week. The Israelites were not to think of it as an onerous requirement, nor was sabbath obedience to be thought of as a drudge. God understands the needs of His creatures and makes full provision for them in His great mercy and out of His bounty. The weekly rest foreshadowed a much greater and more fulfilling rest in the kingdom. In return, God asks now for trusting dedication. Keeping the sabbath and maintaining the tabernacle ordinances showed honour and respect for God – a respect that should have permeated every part of each Israelite's life.

The blasphemer

We can now see how appropriately the incident of the blasphemous man fits into Leviticus 24. It provides an example of the lack of respect God abhorred, and which He wished His people to abhor as well. The circumstances of the case also provide other important lessons for those who seek to serve God faithfully.

When Israel left Egypt, a mixed multitude accompanied God's people into the wilderness. Many in that mixed multitude must have been of Egyptian origin, and there will have been some cases of intermarriage. The blasphemous man's mother was an Israelite of the tribe of Dan and his father was an Egyptian. In God's dealings with His people He always encouraged "the stranger that is among you" to appreciate the benefits of covenant relationship with Israel's God. The fact that the encouragement was necessary suggests that full integration did not happen naturally, and it is possible that this man's mixed parentage led to criticism and discrimination. Was this perhaps the reason why he "and a man of Israel strove together in the camp" (Leviticus 24:10)? There is no doubt that he cursed Israel's God; he "blasphemed the Name, and cursed" (verse 11, RV). The Authorised Version adds in italics that the name of God was "*the* LORD (Yahweh)", but by referring simply to "the Name" it is apparent the man had belittled all that the covenant name described. It was not simply a profane or thoughtless use of a holy name, dreadful though such abuses can be, but a deliberate belittling of God's power and holiness. The man showed himself to be more than an unbeliever. It was not simply that he placed no confidence in Israel's God; he utterly despised all the claims Israel were asked to uphold about God, and he also despised those who sought to honour Him.

God's name and man's name

What else do we know about the man? Apart from his confrontation with an Israelite and that he had a Jewish mother and an Egyptian father, we only know about the incident of his cursing and blaspheming. Not even his name is recorded, for "the Lord, having saved the people out of the land of Egypt, afterward destroyed them that believed not" (Jude 5). The man paid no regard to God's Name, so God refused to acknowledge his name. We do however learn his mother's name: she was "Shelomith, the daughter of Dibri, of the tribe of Dan" (Leviticus 24:11). There must be a reason why this information has been recorded. Could it be that the names of his Israelite forebears are significant? Shelomith means "peaceful"; Dibri means "my word"; and Dan means "judge". O that the son had learned peacefulness from his mother, and recognised the need to fear the judgement of God's word! Instead he allied himself to his father's people and probably also to their Egyptian gods. As a result, he was placed in custody to await the judgement of God's word.

Was this the first time the third commandment had been broken? It is apparent that the people knew the man had done wrong, but had no instructions about the punishment he should face. The answer received from God was uncompromising, and it was directed as much to the nation as it was to the offender himself. The way this particular case was handled was to be exemplary; a pattern was established to be used by the nation in future cases where God's laws and commandments were broken.

The judicial process

A three-part process was to be followed:

1. the offender was to be brought before all the people in the camp;

2. those who witnessed his sin were to identify themselves with his punishment by laying their hands on his head;

3. finally, the execution by stoning was to be undertaken by "all the congregation".

The reason for selecting stoning as the means of execution was that it involved a number of people and required no special skills. Under this method the offender was killed by the congregation, and not by a single individual. No one would know whose stone delivered the coup de grâce. The congregation therefore took collective responsibility for executing the punishment in such serious cases. In fact, the whole process was judicial and involved the nation as a whole. It militated against anyone trying to arrange a kangaroo court or form a lynch mob. The method prescribed by God was simple, just, and measured.

We may be surprised that Moses and the people needed instruction about the penalty for blasphemy; and it is possible that the doubt was less about the nature of the punishment for blasphemy than about whether Israel's law applied to non-Jews. There is a strong hint of this in Moses' words:

> "He that blasphemeth the name of the LORD, he shall surely be put to death, and all the congregation shall certainly stone him: *as well the stranger, as he that is born in the land.*" (Leviticus 24:16)

A few verses later we read: "Ye shall have one manner of law, as well for the stranger, as for one of your own country" (verse 22).

Not only was this law for strangers and Israelites, the judicial process also applied, as we have suggested, to other potential cases and other crimes, even when the punishment was not necessarily the death penalty. This introduced another important principle. The punishment was to be appropriate to the crime and should never be exceeded:

> "He that killeth any man shall surely be put to death … and if a man cause a blemish in his neighbour; as he

159

hath done, so shall it be done to him; breach for breach, eye for eye, tooth for tooth." (verses 17,19,20)

These verses and others like them have caused many to characterise the Old Testament law as brutal and harsh. The intention however was to limit the desire for revenge that arises naturally when a wrong has been committed. We are not to look at these passages and see only the brutality of "an eye for an eye", but we are to see instead the merciful controls that were introduced to prevent judicial punishment getting out of hand.

A more excellent way

There is an even better way for individuals to act, and the Lord comments on this in his Sermon on the Mount. He reminded his hearers of the law controlling retribution:

"Ye have heard that it hath been said, An eye for an eye, and a tooth for a tooth: but I say unto you, That ye resist not evil … give to him that asketh thee, and from him that would borrow of thee turn not thou away."

(Matthew 5:38-42)

Every day, like the Israelites, we are asked to live in the knowledge of God's holiness, manifesting the qualities that are inherent in His name. As Jesus said: "Be ye therefore merciful, as your Father also is merciful" (Luke 6:36).

22

LIBERTY AND JUBILEE
Leviticus 25

ANY consideration of Israel's religious calendar will soon reveal the importance of the sabbath in the nation's life. The weekly cycle of six days of labour and one day of rest established a template promising an eternal rest when God's purpose with His creation is finally complete. This sabbath pattern extends in Leviticus 25 to two extra observances in the nation's religious calendar. These were different from all the others because they did not occur every year.

Each seventh year, the Israelites were to observe a sabbath of rest. The weekly sabbath was for the benefit of man and beast, whereas the sabbath every seventh year was additionally a "sabbath of rest *unto the land*" (Leviticus 25:4). For this reason, the seventh year could not be kept properly until God's people took possession of the land of promise.

Once in a lifetime

The second additional observance was the year of jubilee, which fell after seven sabbath years were celebrated: i.e., after forty-nine years. A jubilee was therefore likely to fall only once, or at most twice in any person's lifetime. As sabbath years were not kept when Israel was in the wilderness, no jubilee was celebrated until the nation was established in the land. These two observances therefore were strongly connected to Israel as a settled nation, occupying the land given to them by God.

The principle underlying the seventh year was established immediately after Moses received the ten commandments.* He was told to set various judgements before the people, and the first one related to the

---

* Is there an oblique reference to this in Leviticus 25:1 where we are told that God "spake unto Moses in mount Sinai"?

treatment of servants. They were to serve only for six years; and their release in the seventh year required no payment on their behalf: they went out "free for nothing" (Exodus 21:2). The sabbath pattern here is six years of bondage before liberty was granted in the seventh year. For servants, the seventh year was a year of release.

Debts were also to be released during the seventh year, just as God brought Israel out from under Egyptian oppression. By showing this generosity of spirit, "the LORD shall greatly bless thee in the land which the LORD thy God giveth thee for an inheritance to possess it" (Deuteronomy 15:4).

This principle was to extend to the land, and in the process the message about liberty and generosity was reinforced. The sabbath year allowed the land to lie fallow, and the enforced rest made it more productive. Any crop that grew of itself was not considered to be the possession of the farmer only, but the fruit was available for everyone, man and beast alike (Leviticus 25:5-7). The people were being reminded that blessings from God are completely undeserved and not dependent at all on man's labour. As they received freely from God's bounty, they were to show the same generosity in their treatment of others, especially those whose circumstances were straitened.

"The land is mine"

The effect of the sabbath year of release was to reduce both poverty and excessive gain. Each of these conditions can be literally soul-destroying, so that the wise man Agur said, "give me neither poverty nor riches; feed me with food convenient for me" (Proverbs 30:8). This objective also applied to the jubilee and was celebrated after seven seven-year cycles. Its start was announced by a trumpet blast, symbolising an urgent call to all in Israel to apply the jubilee measures appropriate to their particular circumstances. These provisions had specific application to the land, for in Israel land was allocated to tribal families for their use, but the title was God's: "the land shall not be sold for ever: for the land is mine; for ye are strangers and sojourners with me" (Leviticus 25:23). It is as if every family in Israel entered into an automatically renewable fifty-year lease. If an Israelite fell on hard times he could raise money on the land. But the value depended on how many years were left until the jubilee. No ownership passed when the land was mortgaged; the agreement related to a period of tenancy determined by the number of years remaining till the next jubilee. If the man's circumstances improved he could redeem the land at any time, and there was no need to wait until the jubilee. However, if he remained too poor to redeem his land, or if there were no wealthy relatives to act on his behalf, the land would certainly become his again when the jubilee trumpet sounded.

Property and the Levites

These arrangements for ensuring that property did not pass completely out of the control of the tribe to which it was originally allocated did not apply in the case of houses within walled cities. If these were sold, the opportunity for redemption was limited to a period of twelve months, with no reversion in the year of jubilee if the property was not redeemed. If the house was in an unwalled city, the same rules applied as for land in general: at the jubilee it would revert to its original owner. Property belonging to Levites was also treated differently. Because Levi had no tribal territory, their houses were covered by the usual jubilee rule. They always had the right of redemption, and all their property was returned in the year of jubilee, "for the houses of the cities of the Levites are their possession among the children of Israel" (Leviticus 25:33).

The word jubilee, Hebrew *yowbel*, has an uncertain derivation. Some scholars suggest it is an onomatopoeic word indicating joy and rejoicing. There would indeed be great rejoicing throughout Israel when the jubilee trumpet was blown and each family entered again into its rightful inheritance. Another suggestion is that the word is based on the root word *yabal* meaning to bear or carry along, expressing the idea that the people were being led by God out of bondage and into His rest (see its use in Exodus 19:13). The sound was to be "sent abroad ... throughout all your land" (Leviticus 25:9, RV), suggesting that a sequence of trumpeters would sound the jubilee, with the blast rippling outwards from Jerusalem to the

163

farthest borders of Israel. No wonder the apostle catches the echo of this once-in-a-lifetime release and speaks of the Lord's return to call his people from the grave "with the trump of God" (1 Thessalonians 4:16). Like that great day of release from the snares of death, each man and woman would enter into God's rest.

A further suggestion links the word with the Phoenician word *ybl*, meaning ram, leading to the translation "trumpets of *rams'* horns" in Joshua 6:4-13. The great joyful blast was sounded on the Day of Atonement, though it is not clear if this happened every year or only at the jubilee.

God's providence

A great measure of faith was required during both the seventh year and the jubilee. Some in Israel, learning that the land was not to be sown during the seventh year, would say: "What shall we eat the seventh year?" (Leviticus 25:20). God promised to give them abundant harvests in the sixth year, whose produce would sustain them during the seventh year, and during the eighth year when the land was planted again to produce fruit for the ninth year. They would surely remember the interpretation of Pharaoh's dream, and Joseph's advice about careful stewardship during the seven years of plenty (Genesis 41:33-36). The effect of that great famine in Egypt was to reduce everyone to the same level of dependence. The Egyptians sold themselves and their lands to Pharaoh, who graciously allowed them to retain four-fifths of everything the land produced. "Only the land of the priests bought he not; for the priests had a portion assigned them of Pharaoh" (47:22).

We can see in what happened in Egypt a model of the divine arrangement that applied in the land of Israel. But whereas the land of Egypt belonged to Pharaoh, Israel was God's land, and His people were His heirs. The Israelites were to bring freewill offerings to God, and they benefited from His constant care. Because of God's great generosity towards them, they were expected to show similar generosity of spirit towards the poor, the disadvantaged and the stranger. The divine blessings in storehouse and barn are beautifully explained in the opening verses of Leviticus 26: "Your threshing shall reach unto the vintage, and the vintage shall reach unto the sowing time: and ye shall eat your bread to the full, and dwell in your land safely" (Leviticus 26:5).

These blessings extended to include peace and safety from enemies, because they indicated how God was ever present among His people: "I will walk among you, and will be your God, and ye shall be my people" (verse 12). When he quoted this verse in his letter to believers in Corinth, the Apostle Paul explained how God's people should separate themselves completely to Him: "Come out from among them, and be ye separate, saith the Lord, and touch not the unclean thing" (2 Corinthians 6:17, quoting Isaiah 52:11). This passage neatly summarises the message of the book of Leviticus and its call to holiness.

An extra year?

The potential for grumbling because of the concern over food supplies during the fallow years would be neatly counterbalanced by the great benefits that attached to the seventh and fiftieth years. Freedom from debts and slavery would encourage deep thankfulness in Israelite hearts. The even greater liberties of the jubilee year could counterbalance the potentially greater privations of a longer period of dependence upon God for supplies of food. We have to ask the question, did the jubilee coincide with a sabbath year, or was it an additional year? After the Exodus, Israel's year started with a remembrance of Passover: "This month (i.e., Abib) shall be unto you the beginning of months: it shall be the first month of the year to you" (Exodus 12:2). The nation thus had two ways of marking the calendar. The religious year commenced at the beginning of Abib, and the civil or agricultural year started with the seventh month Tisri. The sabbath year, which was related to the agricultural cycle yet had a deeply religious significance, could have started at either time. The scriptures do not provide clear evidence one way or the other. The feast of trumpets at the beginning of the seventh month would be an appropriate occasion to mark the start of a year of release, as would the celebration of Passover during the first month.

In either case – during the first month or at the beginning of the seventh month – it is very unlikely that the seventh sabbath year started at the same time as the jubilee trumpet sounded. The jubilee started on "the tenth day of the seventh month, in the day of atonement" (Leviticus 25:9), making it abundantly apparent that there can be no true liberty while sin still reigns. This means that the jubilee year did not completely coincide with the year of release; there was "slippage" of at least ten days, and possibly of half a year between the two celebrations. This helps to explain why the jubilee is described as occurring *after* forty-nine years, and why Israel would "hallow the *fiftieth* year" (verse 10).

Generosity to servants

The jubilee was undoubtedly a super-sabbath year. When the trumpet sounded all slaves were released; any land that had been sold during the previous forty-nine years reverted to the seller or his family; and all debts were cancelled. This was a wonderfully enlightened system, so different from what Israel knew in Egypt, or what was commonplace in Canaan. It caused there to be a completely different attitude towards slavery. God recognised that a man or woman falling on hard times would have to seek employment from wealthier neighbours. But they were not to take advantage of his poverty by making him a bondservant. They could not own him, for he was one of God's covenant people. He was to be treated instead as a hired servant, and given his liberty in the jubilee year (verses 39,40).

There is no doubt that the sabbath year and the jubilee were intended to inculcate in the people of Israel an attitude of thankfulness and generosity. It fostered a truly Utopian society based on an acknowledgement of God's supremacy. If they remembered what they had been redeemed from in Egypt, how could they rule over any of their brethren "with rigour" (verse 43, cp. Exodus 1:13,14)? And whereas Jews were allowed to enslave those of other nations, and even to bequeath their slaves to subsequent generations, they were not to treat their brethren in that way (Leviticus 25:45,46). The law also provided for a situation where an Israelite sold himself to one of another race. His relatives could redeem him at any time, with the redemption price being calculated on the basis of the number of years left until the next jubilee. If he was not redeemed, he would in any case go free in the jubilee year, because "unto me", God said, "the children of Israel are servants … whom I brought forth out of the land of Egypt" (Leviticus 25:55).

23

PERFECTING HOLINESS
Leviticus 26,27

IN common with other parts of the Law of Moses, the book of Leviticus includes in its closing chapters the promise of blessings if Israel was obedient, and the consequences that would flow if the people were disobedient. The chapter of blessings and curses that is best known is Deuteronomy 28, where only 14 of the 68 verses refer to blessings. The same disparity exists in Leviticus 26. Blessings are listed in verses 1-13, and the remainder of the chapter is devoted to punishments. This suggests very strongly that attempts to encourage Israel to be a holy nation would not succeed, and that most people would succumb to worldly attractions and fail to rise to the holiness revealed to them in God's character.

These blessings and curses are introduced in Leviticus 26 by a short description of three simple principles that, if they were followed, would draw men and women closer to God. They summarise and build upon the ten commandments: "make no idols ... keep my sabbaths ... reverence my sanctuary" (Leviticus 26:1,2). Whereas some commentators view these verses as an unwarranted intrusion into the text, there is every reason to see them as a helpful introduction to the consequences of either following or refusing to follow the guidance given in God's law.

True holiness is impossible when men and women construct or worship idols that are the work of men's hands. As Jesus himself declared, "ye cannot serve God and mammon" (Matthew 6:24). A life of service before God, and recognition that every part of life must reflect the coming day of rest, draws men and women to God and away from wickedness.

The addition to the ten commandments is the reference to the sanctuary. When the commandments were first given, the tabernacle details had not been revealed. Indeed, the tabernacle was required because the people specifically asked God, through Moses, not to speak directly to them again but to communicate through representatives (Exodus 20:19).

Blessings

Those who live in harmony with God, "walk in (His) statutes and keep (His) commandments" (Leviticus 26:3). For His part, God promised to respond when the nation of Israel practised holiness. He promised a fruitful and productive land (verses 4,5) and peace from enemy nations (verses 6-8). This blessing on the land reflects God's promised care during the year of release. Just as the sixth year's harvest would supply the nation's needs until the land produced again in the ninth year (25:22), so "the vintage shall reach unto the sowing time: and ye shall eat your bread to the full" (26:5).

These wonderful blessings encouraged the faithful in Israel, and they formed the basis of descriptions of the final blessings God will bring upon His people through the work of the Lord Jesus Christ. In such well known Messianic prophecies as Psalm 72 and Isaiah 11, for example, there are references and echoes drawn from Leviticus 26:3-13. But it is probably the prophet Ezekiel who relies most strongly on this passage in the law, so that some critics have suggested that the whole of what we have called 'the Law of Holiness' (Leviticus 18–27) was written in Ezekiel's day and added to material from another source.* Such a view fails to take account of the integrity of Leviticus which we have been able to see throughout this study. Ezekiel draws on these blessings and relates them to the culmination of God's purpose because only through the obedience of Christ can God's people fully receive the blessings He promised.

If the people of Israel would walk with God, He would walk with them: "I will walk among you, and will be your God" (Leviticus 26:12). The Apostle Paul quotes this

---

* See, for example, *An Introduction to the Pentateuch*, A T Chapman (Cambridge Bible for Schools and Colleges), Appendix V, pages 240-255.

passage in 2 Corinthians 6:16, when he tells believers in Christ not to be "unequally yoked together with unbelievers" or indulge in idolatry and the immorality that was always associated with it. He saw God's promise as a great call to His people to come to Him: "I will receive you, and will be a Father unto you, and ye shall be my sons and daughters" (2 Corinthians 6:17,18; cp. Isaiah 52:11).

There can be no doubt that the theme of Leviticus underlies the Apostle's argument in Corinthians, for he goes on to say in extremely telling words:

"Having therefore these promises, dearly beloved, let us cleanse ourselves from all filthiness of the flesh and spirit, *perfecting holiness* in the fear of God."

(2 Corinthians 7:1)

The objective of all the regulations in Leviticus that seem so pernickety and alien to our modern way of life was that men and women should appreciate on a daily basis how easy it is to stray from God's ways. If, by thinking of the dangers of physical uncleanness it was possible to be more aware of the dangers of moral defilement, it may help individuals to make a concerted effort to cleanse their minds.

While the provisions of the law no longer apply to us, and while they seem strange to the twenty-first century mind, the underlying objective remains true even today. We are no less liable to moral defilement, and there is as much idolatry and immorality in today's world as ever there was in Egypt or Canaan when the message of Leviticus was given to Moses.

The promised blessings rarely occurred in the history of Israel. The experience of the nation is more accurately described in the list of negative consequences that would follow Israel's failure to apply God's word or heed His advice. We therefore find in verses 14-39 Israel's sad history written in advance.

Punishments

The punishments are all introduced by a telling phrase: "If ye will not hearken unto me ..." (verses 14,18,21,23,27). This was the basis for the divine judgements that would

170

	Nature of punishment	Examples of fulfilment in Israel's history
26:14-17	General warnings	Jeremiah 5:17; Micah 6:15
26:18-20	Drought and poor harvest	Haggai 1:10,11
26:21,22	Danger from wild animals	1 Samuel 17:34-36 2 Kings 17:25,26
26:23-26	Wars	Judges 2:11-15; 2 Kings 17:18-20
26:27-39	Siege and exile	Jeremiah 9:16; Ezekiel 5:10-14

follow. Those judgements were also to have a degree of intensity: "I will punish you seven times more for your sins" (verses 18,21,24,28). The expression "seven times more" probably means a punishment completely answering the sin, rather than one where the punishment exceeds the crime sevenfold.* But it would also remind the Israelites of God's covenant, so often expressed in sevens: the seventh day, seventh month, seventh year, etc. His covenant was certain; and equally certain was His proportionate response to sin.

There was another aspect to God's judgements, and this comes out most clearly in Ezekiel 20, where the prophet reflects on the history of God's dealings with Israel. He speaks of the people not walking in God's statutes, despising His judgements and polluting His sabbaths (Ezekiel 20:13,16,21,24). Yet for all this, God said: "mine eye spared them from destroying them, neither did I make an end of them in the wilderness" (verse 17). Such was the effect of God's covenant with Israel. His mercy and grace would be extended to the nation, though only to the faithful remnant:

* Cf. Genesis 4:15: "Whosoever slayeth Cain, vengeance shall be taken on him sevenfold", meaning that the murderer would not escape unpunished; and Daniel 3:19, where the increased intensity of the burning fiery furnace probably means that the furnace was heated to the full extent of its ability.

"I will for their sakes remember the covenant of their ancestors, whom I brought forth out of the land of Egypt in the sight of the heathen, that I might be their God: I am the Lord." (Leviticus 26:45)

Such gracious treatment was dependent on the people confessing their iniquity, and acknowledging that they had walked contrary to God's ways. Leviticus 26 therefore concludes with a section reminding Israel of how God will never forget His covenant with Israel, and will show His mercy towards them:

"I will not cast them away (cf. Romans 11:2), neither will I abhor them, to destroy them utterly, and to break my covenant with them: for I am the Lord their God." (Leviticus 26:44)

Concluding statements

This is a very fitting thought on which to conclude the book, and indeed the last verse of the chapter rounds everything off by saying:

"These are the statutes and judgments and laws, which the Lord made between him and the children of Israel in mount Sinai by the hand of Moses." (verse 46)

But Leviticus contains another chapter that concludes with almost identical words (cp. 27:34), and this has confused many commentators who wonder why it was included. Various suggestions have been made. Some believe that it simply explains the next law that was given to Moses in Sinai, and that we are not to be concerned with its position in the book. Another view holds that it was a much later addition, and was simply added on at the end.

Yet neither of these suggestions provides a satisfactory explanation of why the chapter occupies the final part of the book of Leviticus. It is possible that the theme of the book supplies the answer. God's call to His people was "be ye holy, for I am holy" (11:44,45; cf. 1 Peter 1:16), and their worship and daily activities were intended to draw them closer to Him and to each other. What could faithful men and women do who contemplated God's holiness? The law made certain demands, but even if it was followed diligently, the individual only did his duty as a member of

God's nation. Was there anything he could do that was above and beyond duty – beyond even the freewill offerings that could be taken to the tabernacle?

Yes, the man could do what the message in Leviticus always urged him to do. He could sanctify himself to God, or he could sanctify his animals, his house, or his fields. He could make a "*singular* vow" – the word means a 'special' or 'hard' vow – promising to give something of his own fully and completely to God. Whatever he sanctified would become "holy unto the LORD", just as God demanded (Leviticus 27:14,21,28,30,32).

Law of redemption

Recognising that what a man promised might also be necessary for the proper execution of his own affairs, the law provided that the sanctified gift could be redeemed on the payment of an appropriate sum of money into the tabernacle treasury. The details are shown in the table below; the sums being based on the estimated productivity of each category of person (Leviticus 27:3-7).

There was also a provision in the law if the person wishing to redeem his vow was not able to pay the full valuation. In such circumstances, the priests could reduce the figure in accordance with the man's ability to pay (verse 8).

In the case of animals, it depended whether the animal was clean and suitable for one of the offerings, or unclean because of some deficiency. A clean animal offered as a sanctified gift could not be redeemed (verse 10); an unclean animal, however, could be redeemed on payment of its estimated value plus a fifth part (verses 11-13). This would remind the person redeeming the animal of the

	Male	Female
1 month – 5 years	5 shekels	3 shekels
5-20 years	20 shekels	10 shekels
20-60 years	50 shekels	30 shekels
60 years and more	15 shekels	10 shekels

trespass offering, where "he shall make amends for the harm that he hath done in the holy thing, and shall add the fifth part thereto" (5:16). The same provision applied in the case of a house that was sanctified to God by a special vow, and even to the tithes that God demanded of His people. They could only be redeemed by paying the estimated value, plus a fifth (Leviticus 27:14,15,31).

The act of sanctification acknowledged that God responds to those who recognise their true destiny. When a man was conscious of his sin, he brought appropriate offerings to indicate his remorse, and undertook generous repayment in case of damage or loss. God promised in these circumstances to accept the offering and the man was regarded as cleansed from his sin. Sanctification only applied in cases where an individual was cleansed from sin. The man or woman had to be in a right relationship with God before sanctifying self or possessions to His service.

When a person dedicated land to God, he had to recognise that the land was not his; he had the land on a renewable tenancy agreement lasting for fifty years until the jubilee. To redeem the land he dedicated, he had to pay its value calculated on the basis of its productivity (plus one-fifth extra), and depending how many years remained until the jubilee. If he did not redeem the land before the jubilee, "the field ... shall be holy unto the LORD, as a field devoted" (verse 21).

Devoted to God

Wherever we turn in this matter of vowing to sanctify something to God, there is a reminder that anything given to Him becomes holy. Yet there are a couple of verses in Leviticus 27 that on the surface create a problem. Items sanctified, or made holy to God, by special vow could generally be redeemed, as we have seen. But there were situations where the law of redemption was disallowed: "no devoted thing ... shall be sold or redeemed ... but shall surely be put to death" (verses 28,29). The two terms "sanctified" and "devoted" are different. To devote something is to hand over without reservation. Therefore, something sanctified could be redeemed, but something devoted remained with God for ever. This was the

174

situation of Jephthah's daughter (Judges 11:31), and no redemption was possible for her. She could either remain wholly with God, or "be put to death".

Here is the climax of holiness; all the regulations in Leviticus build up to this great truth. The law recognised that the pursuit of holiness was dogged by man's mortality; he was always being dragged down by submitting to earthly lusts. True and complete devotion to God will only be possible for sinful man when he is freed from sin. If he cannot remain with God for ever, as Christ did, he must die to sin in order that he might live to God:

"No flesh should glory in (God's) presence. But of him are ye in Christ Jesus, who of God is made unto us wisdom, and righteousness, and sanctification, and redemption." (1 Corinthians 1:29,30)

SUBJECT INDEX

Aaronic priesthood, failure of, 23, 116

Abhorent practices, 128

Aholiab, 2

Amalek, war with, 1

Ammon and Moab, origin of, 138

Analysis, Leviticus 19, 133

Ananias and Sapphira, 83

"And He Called", Jewish title for Leviticus, 15

Animal sacrifice, alien to present way of life, 27

Anniversary, first, 2

Anointing with oil, 79, 87

Atonement, day of, 116, 148; summary of details, 123

Azazel, 120

Balanced view of sacrifice, 36

Bathsheba, David's sin with, 37, 54

Bezaleel, 2

Blasphemer of God's name, 7, 21, 24, 157

Blasphemy, punishment for, 158

Blessings and curses, 168

Blood, shedding of, 40; not to be eaten, 125

Bread and Wine, 73

Bread from heaven, 1

Burning Bush, 8, 13

Burnt offering, continual, 57; details, 51; national, 57; personal, 58; summary, 58

Calendar, religious, 146

Camp, arrangement, 3

Canaan, idolatrous, 125

Census, 3

Cereal (meal) offering, 27

Ceremony, inauguration, 79

Chata'ah (sin offering), 31

Child sacrifice, 129, 137

Childbirth, ritually defiling, 105

Chiun (god Saturn), 129

Christ Jesus, law fulfilled in him, 16, 55

Christendom's curse, 121

Clean, 11, 92, 98

Cloud, pillar of, 13

Commitment, wholehearted, 32

Common, 9, 92

Consecration, of Aaron and sons, 7, 21

Convocations, holy, 149

Covenant of salt, 72

Cursing of parents, 138

Cyclical worship, 4, 146

Dates, absence of, 3

David, sin with Bathsheba, 37, 54

Day of Atonement, 21, 116, 148; summary of details, 123

Deceit and violence, 49

Defilement, 99
Devoted things, 174
Dialogue, God–Moses–People, 21
Dietary laws, reasons for, 90; summary of, 97
Discharges, sexual, summary of laws relating to, 103
Discharges, bodily, 99
Disciples, plucking ears of corn, 151, 156
Dispensation, Christian, 16; Mosaic, 16
Drink offering, 27, 72

Ecclesia, 149; in the wilderness, 83
Egypt, idolatrous, 125
Eleazar, 88
Eli, 89
Erroneous idea, substitution, 122
Euphemisms for sexual intercourse, 128

Fat, burning of, 41, 61
Feast of Pentecost, 64
Fellowship, with God, 62; meal, 80
Firstfruits, 151
Frankincense, 70
Fruit, not to harvest for 3 years, 136

Gifts for sanctuary, 2
God's call, 15
Gods of nature, 125
Golden Calf, sin in matter of, 13, 77

Hallow, (verb), 8
Harvest, 152
Heave thigh (shoulder), 60
Hebrews, link with Leviticus, 17

Historical events, only three, 3, 7, 21; relate to holiness, 7
Holiness, in family life, 133; Law of, summary, 145; of believers in Christ, 6; of God, 5; of priests, 6; theme of Leviticus, 20, 132; understanding, 7, 11
Holy, day, 7; ground, 7; Name, God's, 8; of Holies, 9; One of Israel, 8; One, Jesus, 11
Honesty pays, 46
Hophni and Phinehas, 89

Idolatrous practices to be shunned, 136
Inauguration ceremony, 79
Instructions regarding sacrifices compared (for people and for priests), 27
Ithamar, 88

Jealousy offering, 69
Jephthah's daughter, 175
Jerusalem Conference, 130
Jesus Christ, law fulfilled in him, 16, 55
Jubilee and Sabbath year, do they coincide? 165
Jubilee, year of, 148, 162

Key words in Leviticus, 12
Korah, Dathan and Abiram, 84

Laid in order, 55
Lampstand, 153; oil for, 154
Law of Moses, doomed to failure, 25; holy, just and good, 25
Leprosy, cleansing, 112; deadly disease, 106; in clothing and houses, 108; signs of, 109; sufferer restored, 113; summary of laws regarding, 115
Lessons, for disciples, 34

Leviticus Chapter19, analysis, 133

Leviticus, analysis 22; origin of name, 15

Lord Jesus Christ, law fulfilled in him, 16, 55

Lot's daughters, 138

Mammon, 130

Marriage relationships, priestly restrictions, 142; prohibited, 126

Mars, 130

Meal Offering, 67

Minchah (cereal offering), 30, 67

Mingling fibres, seeds, 135

Mishael and Elzaphan, 87

Moab and Ammon, origin of, 138

Moloch (Molech), 129, 137

Moses, as priest, 78; excluded from Tabernacle, 15; God's messenger, 13

Nadab and Abihu, death of, 7; presumption of, 83; prophetic, 24; sin of, 21, 116

Nearness of God, in Christ, 19; in Tabernacle, 18

Neighbour, to be loved, 5

Numbers, linked with Leviticus, 16

Offerings, 4 major, relevant for today, 30; grouped in pairs, 27; jealousy, 69; order of, 28; powerless to remove sin, 35; requirements appropriate to status, 38; summary chart, 28; voluntary, 51

Oil, anointing, 79, 87

Olah (burnt offering), 31

Omer, of manna, 69

Ornan the Jebusite, 55

Pan, Greek god, 125

Parents, cursing equivalent to blasphemy, 138; bring children in subjection to God, 133, 144

Passover (feast Unleavened bread), 150; night, 1

Peace offering, 59; alternative translations, 59; as a freewill offering, 62; as a thanksgiving, 62; resulting from a vow, 62

Pentecost, Feast of, 64

Phrases, repeated in Leviticus Chapter 23, 147

Pillar of Cloud, 13

Powerless to remove sin, 35

Preparation, of sacrificial animal, 53

Priesthood, intrinsic weakness, 24; inauguration, 75

Priests, critical role, 20, 23; failure of, 23; representation, 75; requirements of, 139; teachers, 20, 23, 143

Profane, 10

Psoriasis, 106

Punishments, national fulfiied, 171

Purpose, of Leviticus, 5, 17

Quaked greatly, 2

Qualifications, priests, 94, 140

Quarantine, 107

Red Sea, 1

Remphan, 129

Representation by priests, 75

Robbing God, 47

Robes, clean linen, 120

Royal Law, 6, 135

Sabbath, importance of, 161; year and Jubilee, do they

coincide? 165; year of release, 161

Sacrifice, of children, 129, 137

Sacrifices, dual purpose, 35;
various methods, 39

Salt, 71

Sanctify (verb), 8

Sardis, 108

Saturn, 129

Satyrs, 125

Savour, sweet, 52

Scapegoat, 121

Separation, 139

Sermon on the Mount, 160

Seven times more, 171

Seven, number, emphasis on,
152

Shalom (peace), 60

Shelomith, 158

Shewbread 69, 155; Ahimelech
gave David, 156

Sin offering, details, 38; for the
poor, 68; frankincense not
included, 69; offered first, 28;
summary of offerings, 52

Sin, defiling and degrading, 13

Sinai, Mount, 1, 78, 84

Sinner, habitual, no provision
for under Law, 37

Sixth year of bounty, 169

Slaves, 135

Stoning, 159

Strong drink, 72, 86

Substitution, erroneous idea,
122

Super-sabbath, 166

Sweet savour, 52

Synagogue, 149

Tabernacle, Moses' 14;
Sanctuary, 14

Ten commandments, 132, 168

Tent, Moses', 14

Third day, 134

Tongue, unruly, 93

Trespass offering, details, 43;
ram always required, 44

Trespass, by a leper, 47;
restitution, 45; restitution by
a disciple of Christ, 48

Trespasses, impact on third
party, 44; relation to sins, 43

Tyndale, coined word "scapegoat", 121

Unclean, 11, 92, 98; warning
cry, 110

Unholy, 9

Unleavened bread, feast
(Passover), 150

Violence and deceit, 49

Voluntary offerings, 51

Vows, 173

Vows, cost of redemption, 173

Water from the rock, 1

Wave breast, 60

Waw conjunctive, 16

Without the Camp, 13, 99

Woman with issue of blood, 104

Words, important, 12

Workmanship, skilled, 2

Yahweh, 157

Zebach (peace offering), 30

Zechariah's vision, 112

SCRIPTURE REFERENCES

Genesis
2:3 8
:17 95
3:19 155
:7 128
:7,21 108
:21 41
4:15 171
8:20,21 52
19:36 138
22:7 57
41:33-36 164
47:22 164
48:17 80

Exodus
1:13,14 166
3:5 8
6:23 84
12:2 . . . . . .25, 165
:16 149
:18 4
:26-28 150
13:11-16 46
14:13 1
:29,31 1
15:17 14
:26 91
16:1 4
:2,3 1
:35 1
:36 69
17:6 1
:16 1
19:1 4
:4-6 1
:6 . . . .47, 75, 113
:13 163
:16,18 2
20:7 135
:10 148
:19 . . . . .13, 169

:26 128
21:2 162
22:1 46
23:14-17 149
24:1-11 84
:2 84
25:2 2
:8 . . . . .2, 14
:40 14
25:–30: 78
28:2 87
:40 122
:42 128
29:19,20 80
:38-42 51
:41 53
:42 57
:43 19
:43-45 77
30:7-9 85
32:4 81
:31,34 13
:32 77
33:7-11 13
:9 13
:11 85
34:6 5
35:3 148
:31 3
:34 3
35:–39: 78
40:17 . . . . .3, 4, 119
:34 14
:35 15

Leviticus
1:–5: 75
1:–7: 28
1:1 . . . . .14, 15, 20
:1,2 17
:14 52
1:1–6:7 27

:2 23
:3 . . . . . . .51, 52
:3-17 28
:5 41
:8,12 56
:9 54
:9,13,17 52
:10 52
2:1-16 . . . . .28, 68
:13 . . . . . .71, 72
:14 70
3:1-17 28
:3-5 60
:9-11 60
:14-16 . . . .31, 60
4:1 20
:1–5:19 28
:2 37
:3 . . . . . . .38, 39
:3,13,14 81
:6,17 39
:7,18 39
:8-12 39
:13 37
:13,14 38
:22,23 38
:25 . . . . . .39, 40
:27,28 38
5:7 38
:11 38
:11-13 68
:14 20
:14-19 44
:15 . . . . . .45, 46
:15,18 44
:16 . . . . . .45, 174
6:1-7 . . . . .28, 44
:1,8,19,24 20
:2 49
:2,3 43
:6 44

180

:8,9 23
:8-13 28
:8–7:38 27
:9 57
:12 61
:14-18 28
:20 69
:23 69
:26 45
7:1-10 28
:2 45
:6 45
:7 . . . . . . .30, 44
:8 53
:11-34 28
:12,13 60
:15-19 63
:20 63
:22,28 20
:30 61
:31-34 60
8:1 20
:3 76
:4 84
:6 79
:6-36 21
:7-9 79
:10-12 79
:22 80
:23,24 113
:31 80
8:–10: 75
9:2 81
:3 88
:6 . . . . . . .81, 84
:8,12 83
:12-21 81
:22 81
:23,24 . . . . .82, 83
10: 116
:1 84
:1-7 21
:3 . . . . . .86, 116
:4 85
:6 110
:7 87
:9 86
:9,10 24
:9-11 . . . . .20, 73
:10 . . . . . .10, 90
:10,11 87

:17 88
:19 . . . . . .83, 88
:20 88
11:1 20
:1,2 90
:1-47 24
:2-8 94
:20-23 94
:24,25 95
:32 96
:32-35 96
:33 96
:39 95
:44 . . . . .5, 7, 90
:44,45 172
:45 . . . . . . .5, 96
11:–15: 90, 93
12: 93, 99, 102
:1 20
:2 101
:7 101
12:–15: 90
13: 108, 109
:1 20
:2-17 110
:3,5,6,8 109
:18-28 110
:29-44 110
:44 110
:45,46 110
:46 . . . . .47, 110
:51 111
13:,14: 93, 111
14: 109
:1,33 20
:7 112
:12 47
:33 20
:40-42 111
:45 112
15: 93, 99,
. . . 100, 102, 108
:1 20
:1-15 100
:3 100
:13 103
:16-18 100
:18 102
:18,19 101
:19-24 100
:21-23 101

:25-30 100
:31 105
16:1 . . . . .18, 20, 21,
. 116
:2 117
:6 120
:8 . . . . . .120, 121
:12,13 85
:16 . . . . .118, 122
:17 120
:22 . . . . .121, 122
:23,24 122
:29 . . . . .118, 119,
. . . . 122
:30,31 119
:33 117
17: 124
:1 20
:1-6 59
:2 21
:2-4 95
:3,4 130
:4,9 125
:5 125
:7 125
:10,14 130
:13 130
:14 125
17:,18: 129, 130
18: 128
:1 20
:2 23
:3 126
:5 131
:6-17 126
:6-23 130
:17,18 128
:19 . . . . .127, 128
:20 128
:21 128
:22 128
:22,23 128
:23 128
:24,25 129
18:–20: 139
18:–27: . . .146, 169
19: 135
:1 20
:2 . . .5, 131, 132,
. 139
:3 . . .18, 133, 138

181

THE BEAUTY OF HOLINESS

Leviticus – *continued*
19:3-10 132
:4 . . . . . .133, 134
:5-10 . . .133, 134
:11,12 133
:11-18 132
:12 135
:13,14 133
:15,16 133
:17,18 133
:18 6
:19-25 133
:19-37 132
:20-22 136
:25 136
:26-28 133
:29,30 133
:31 133
:32 133
:32-37 136
:33,34 133
:35-37 133
19:,20: 32
20: 136, 138
:1 20
:1-5 137
:5 137
:6 137
:7 139
:9 . . . . .137, 138
:10 137
:11,12,17-21 . .137
:13,15,16 137
:14 . . . . .138, 143
:24-26 92
:26 . . . . . .5, 132
:27 . . . .137, 138
21:1 . . . . .139, 141
:1-8 140
:2,3 87
:6 . . . . . .18, 139
:7 142
:8 139
:9 142
:10-12 . . .86, 141
:10-15 140
:13,14 142
:15,23 139
:16 20
:16-23 140
:21 140

:5,6,17-23 94
21:,22: 139
22:1-16 140
:1,17,26 20
:10-16 143
:16,32 139
:17-33 140
:20 140
:20-25 140
:23 63
23: 146, 153
:1-3 146
:1,9,23,26,33 . .20
:2 146
:2,4,37,44 147
:2,4,7,8,21,24,27,
35,37 147
:3 147
:4-14 146
:4-22 146
:7 147
:7,8,21,25,28,30,
31,36 147
:11 151
:13 70
:15-22 146
:16 70
:17 151
:19 65
:22 151
:22,43 146
:23-32 146
:23-44 146
:27 119
:29 120
:32 148
:39-44 152
:40 152
24: . . .153, 154, 157
:1,13 20
:1-4 154
:2,3 154
:3 155
:5-9 . . . . .70, 155
:8 156
:10 157
:10,11 24
:10-12 21
:11 . . . .157, 158
:16 159
:17,19,20 160

:22 159
25: . .148, 153, 154,
. 161
:1 . . . . . .20, 161
:4 161
:5-7 162
:9 . .123, 163, 166
:10 166
:20 164
:22 169
:23 162
:33 163
:39,40 166
:43 166
:45,46 166
:55 167
26: 165, 168
:1,2 168
:1-13 168
:3 169
:4,5 169
:5 . . . . .165, 169
:6-8 169
:12 . . . .165, 169
:14,18,21,23,27 . .
. 170
:14-17 171
:14-39 170
:18,21,24,28 . .171
:18-20 171
:21,22 171
:23-26 171
:27-39 171
:44 172
:45 172
:46 172
27:1 20
:3-7 173
:8 173
:10 173
:11-13 173
:14,15,31 174
:14,21,28,30,32 . .
. 173
:21 174
:27 46
:28,29 174
:34 . . . . . . .4, 172
Numbers
1:1 . . .3, 4, 16, 119
5:11-31 69

182

5:12,27 44
6:12 48
:24-27 81
8:7 113
9:6,7 87
10:10 58
:11 4
12:12 106
15:1-15 67
:1-16 28
18:12,29,30,32 . . .61
28:3 57
:5 68
:7 72
29:7-11 122
Deuteronomy
6:5 57
:6-9 144
12:20-25 59, . . .124
:7 60
15:4 162
23:12-14 99
:14 13
26:10 68
28: 168
Joshua
6:4-13 164
Judges
11:31 175
2:11-15 171
1 Samuel
2:35 89
6:4 44
15:22 31
16:7 53
17:34-36 171
21:5 156
:6 156
1 Kings
11:7 137
2 Kings
5:14 113
:18 130
17:18-20 171
:25,26 171
1 Chronicles
21:24 55
24:2 84
2 Chronicles
17:11 67
24:18 44

Psalms
14:3 33
22:14 31
32:1,2 123
35:13,14 119
40: 31, 33, 34
:6 30
:7 33
:7,8 31
:8 34
50:13-15 64
:23 63
51:1,2 37
:5 102
:6 32
:6,17 38
:10 54
:16 37
:19 54
72: 169
89:18 8
103:12 121
116:17,18 64
119:105 155
133:1,2 79
Proverbs
30:8 162
Isaiah
6:3 9
:5 9
7:15,16 93
11: 169
38:17 121
42:2,3 49
52:11 . . . . .165, 170
53:6 121
:9,10 49
:10 . . . . . .42, 49
:12 . . . . . .42, 73
55:8,9 9
57:5 137
:15 9
Jeremiah
5:17 171
9:16 171
19:5 137
Ezekiel
5:10-14 171
20:13,16,21,24 . .171
20:17 171
24:15-18 141

24:17 110
28:24 111
40:26 52
Amos
4:2 8
5:25-27 129
6:8 8
Daniel
3:19 171
Hosea
4:8,9 89
:9 2 5
6:6 . . . . . . .31, 35
Jonah
2:9 64
Micah
6:6,7 33
:15 171
Haggai
1:10,11 171
Zechariah
5:4 112
Malachi
2:6,7 88
:7 143
Matthew
3:17 42
5:38-42 160
:48 . . . . . . .5, 90
6:2 58
:11 155
:14,15 43
:24 168
7:23 93
8:2,3 114
9:20-22 104
11:28 148
12:3,7,8 157
:31 37
13:39 70
18:35 50
19:19 . . . . . .6, 135
22:39 . . . . . .6, 135
Mark
2:27 8
7:15 91
:19 91
9:49 72
:50 72
12:31 135
:32,33 57

Luke
1:35 11
6:1 151
:5 151
:36 . . . . . .5, 160
10:27 135
12:48 . . . . .39, 139
16:10 98
John
1:14 19
:29 . . . . . .34, 39
4:34 . . . . . .29, 73
6:63 41
11:39 134
Acts
2:1 65
:5,41,42 65
3:14,15 11
5:1-11 83
7:42,43 129
10:28 92
15: 145
15:1 130
15:28,29 130
17:27,28 18
Romans
1:4 11
3:23 . . . . . .43, 51
4:7,8 123
5:12 . . .41, 93, 106
:19 102
6:6 41
7:12 25
:12,13 48
:13 93
8:3 . . . . . .25, 104
10:5 131
:6 131
11:2 172
12:1 . . . .32, 55, 56
1 Corinthians
1:29 41
:29,30 175
7:14 143
9:13 40
10:4 1

11:22 135
15:20 65
:3,4 151
:33 104
:46 98
2 Corinthians
4:6 . . . . . . .19, 81
6:16 170
:17 165
:17,18 170
7:1 170
Galatians
3:12 131
:24 . . . . . .vii, 142
5:19-21 37
Ephesians
2:8 46
4:29 72
Philippians
2:17 73
Colossians
2:23 131
3:2 56
4:6 72
1 Thessalonians
4:16 164
1 Timothy
2:15 104
3:3 86
:11,12 143
:15 109
Titus
1:6 143
Hebrews
1:1,2 17
:12 37
2:14 76
:17 76
3:1 81
:5 . . . . . .16, 79
4:9 118
:12 54
:15 114
5:1,2 76
:1-3 81
:3 76

:9 82
6:6 111
7:11 15
:16 24
:28 83
8:5 14
9:8,9 118
:22 . .41, 114, 120
:23,24 9
10: 33
:4 . . . . . . .32, 35
:7,9 33
:10 34
:22 55
:24,25 152
12:9 134
:14 . . . . . .11, 86
:18 13
13:10,11 40
:11 62
:13 40
:15 62
James
1:17 . . . . . .11, 135
2:8 . . . . . . .6, 135
:10 99
3:7,8 93
1 Peter
1:13 – 2:10 6
:16 172
:19 35
2:5 111
1 John
1:9 . . . . . . .29, 48
3:4 43
5:17 38
Jude
:5 158
:23 108
Revelation
2:23 54
7:14 108
13:8 34
14:4 142
19:8 120